Physics of Closed Systems:
Addictions

Holographic Human Open System Experience

Janey Marvin

Physics of Closed Systems: Addictions
Holographic Human Open System Experience

Copyright © 2021 by Janey Marvin.

Paperback ISBN: 978-1-63812-049-0
Hardcover ISBN: 978-1-63812-050-6
Ebook ISBN: 978-1-63812-071-1

All rights reserved. No part in this book may be produced and transmitted in any form or by any means, electronic, or mechanical, including photocopying, recording, or by any information storage and retrieval system, without permission in writing from the copyright owner.

The views expressed in this work are solely those of the author and do not necessarily reflect the views of the publisher hereby disclaims any responsibility for them.

Published by Pen Culture Solutions   07/15/2021

Pen Culture Solutions
1-888-727-7204 (USA)
1-800-950-458 (Australia)
support@penculturesolutions.com

Open vs. Closed System

World View
Quantity and Exponent

DATA
Admit / Deny

INFORMATION
Accept / Refuse

KNOWLEDGE
Express / Repress

Self View
Power and Function

Cycles through limiting beliefs and dysfunctional patterns

INTRODUCTION

Holographic Human Transformation Theory "Physics of Closed Systems" originates from the Holographic Human Theory. Holographic Human Theory incorporates wisdoms of the ancient Greeks and is based upon three simple words at the entrance of the Temple of Delphi: Know Thy Self.

Holographic Human Transformation Theory gives us knowledge of our inner world, our subconscious self which has been directing our lives throughout all mortality. All of our fears, hatred, envying, sorrows, anxieties, everything we thought to be a part of us and the world. Everything we experience as our Reality, Identity. IQ, Emotion, Thought, Physical, all of our being is subconscious programming. The Greek knew this, and they knew the inner-beings Nature: it's Structure, its Patterns and its Processes. Holographic Human Theory and Transformation Theory is research put together from years of research and implementation.

I have studied Holographic Human Theory since 1996 after attending a weekend training from Michael Miller on it. Something about it, I could not put it down. I researched every single word in his book I received from the training that had to do with Holographic Human Theory. Including simple words such as "it", "of", "is", "as". I researched words I had never used before. I researched in dictionaries, thesauruses, scriptures, physics, and quantum physics. I researched Einstein, Max Planck, Thomas Kuhn and many other physicists whose works the research lead me to. My research process consisted of first gathering Data from any and all sources corresponding with my scriptural researching and knowledge. After gathering the Data of each and every word, I took the data of each word and then wrote a dialogue of information from the data of the word and created theories corresponding with the Holographic Human. Lastly, I practiced and applied the information and theories from the data and dialogue and repeated from step one of my research, gathering any new Data I ran into during the implementing stage, this leads to greater knowledge.

This book is one of many books I have written and will continue to write regarding Holographic Human and Holographic Human Transformation Theory because the information is copious.

Holographic Human Theory consists of many different natures of Know Thy Self: Linguistics, CNS neuron-firings, human senses (7) their functions and intelligence each body organ and system and its abstract function and individual intelligence, and the nature all of this corresponds together to make us "Be". Much that is not run by conscious was known by the ancient Greeks and is passed on in the Holographic Human Theory. Holographic Human Theory teaches you to recognize all of these subconscious functions, to know their intelligences, and nature to "Know Thy Self". It teaches you, along with the techniques I have developed based upon their functions, the way to "Heal Thy Self".

All conscious functions are for our "Being" to perceive what subconscious tells it to, to evaluate it, to judge it, and then to decide about it. Everything else, we have known as "Self", is just subconscious programming. Even what conscious gets to perceive "about".

I have done this now since 1996. I have thousands of papers and illustrations; I have taught it as part of our educational class in our treatment facility. I am writing books for other professionals and anyone interested. I have created hundreds of experiential techniques to apply the information more easily in group and individual settings. I do trainings, coaching. I have worked in Human Services since 1976. I have owned and operated my own treatment program since 1993. I received my Master in Hypnotherapy and Certified with the International Medical Dental Hypnotherapy Association in Hypno-anesthesia in 1994. I was one of three people west of the Mississippi certified by them to do Hypno-anesthesia. I had to learn the structure, patterns and processes of brain and body organ and system functions and correspondence and conscious consequences. Already knowing these things then just a weekend training of Holographic Human and I knew there was more of greater value than had been recognized yet.

I love the work I do. I love believing when a person knows the path to help them to become a greater being, they will choose it.

"I believe in God, the Eternal Father and in His Son, Jesus Christ and in the Holy Ghost.", the First Article of Faith of the Church of Jesus Christ of Latter-Day Saints. I believe we are all God's children. I believe it is His work and His glory to "bring to pass the immortality and eternal life of man".

He gave us all the Gospel of Jesus Christ of Latter-Day Saints; He created us to return to Him for immortality and eternal life. I believe "a man cannot be saved in ignorance", D&C 131:6. I believe "If there is anything virtuous, lovely or of good report, we seek after these things", Thirteenth Article of Faith of the Church of Jesus Christ of Latter-Day Saints.

I believe that Lucifer will give you 99 truths to get you to believe 1 lie. The scriptures are a significant resource of my research.

Holographic Human Theory and Holographic Human Transformation Theory teach you about your inner self, the self that has been a mystery to us all for most of our mortality. The consequences of not knowing thy self (our subconscious programs): Is despair, hurt, disease, depression, all the mortal problems whether mental, emotional or physical are the consequences of not knowing our inner self.

This book teaches the purpose and origins of any addiction and walks you step by step through overcoming. Whether the addiction is yours personally or someone you love, the process is the same, the structure and patterns of addiction are always the same.

Editing - Sean Nagel
Editing Assistant - Linda Dimmick
Images and Graphics – Joel Christie

Contents

Chapter 1	Closed Systems Are Addictive Systems	1
Chapter 2	Closed System's Boundaries Are Not Flexible/Permeable	13
Chapter 3	Lost Desires, Dreams, And Goals	23
Chapter 4	Physics Of Addictions	53
Chapter 5	The Cause Of Closed Systems	78
Chapter 6	Open Systems	86
Chapter 7	Time And Addictions	95
Chapter 8	Unbridgeability	106
Chapter 9	Memory And Addictions	112
Chapter 10	Other Effects Of Addictions	120
Chapter 11	Identity And Addictions	125

Chapter 1

CLOSED SYSTEMS ARE ADDICTIVE SYSTEMS

This is not a Twelve Step book, however, there are many references and support groups which can easily be found on the internet and in your local community for 12 Step help. This book is from my experiences, my knowledge, and of course my beliefs.

I say, "Addiction is not just the addict's problem. One person does not an addict alcoholic make. It took a team to get us into our addiction and it takes a team to get us out and keep us out."

I am an addict, my father was an alcoholic, and his father was an alcoholic. The family problem with addiction goes in many different directions on the Family Tree. There is a scripture which I contemplate which states that the sins of the parents are on the heads of the children for four generations. I know, this isn't always the case, if everyone in the genealogy stories are being truthful. I and my siblings do have different traits from both our parents, some are good and some we have worked on to overcome.

The fact of the matter is, no one, no one, just woke up one morning out of a good night's rest, yawned, stretched and thought, "I think I'll become an addict or alcoholic today." Addictions can quickly change from one substance to another. Though, the addiction itself comes from inside of us. No matter what the drug, alcohol, or addiction might be, it just doesn't happen that way. It's a process that happens over a period of time, it's a combination of many different memories, programs, models and beliefs. The common factor to the path of addiction is sympathizing and indulging beliefs contrary to our true self. Sympathizing comes because of a relationship between the persons or a thing where whatever affects one similarly affects the other. This brings about a feeling of loyalty and a tendency to favor or support the other person or thing contrary to our true beliefs. Indulgence indicates a tolerant or a forgiving nature to a point of leniency giving free rein to others to a point of excess. These tolerance and indulging's of contrary beliefs can start very innocently in their outward appearance, as just poor choices. Poor choices we are totally consciously convinced are the right choice even though they are contrary of our true self. A Closed System is more likely to be making poor choices this way than an Open System. A Closed System is more likely to sympathize and indulge to a point of excess. I am speaking of contrary to our own true beliefs, beliefs we are consciously aware of and value. A Closed System is more likely to go contrary to their true self inner beliefs than an Open System. The environment is the trigger to the poor choice and the perception of the environment is what is really necessary for the true self to grow. The way the individual perceives the environment is the main factor in triggering the Closed System response. Closed Systems view the environment in specific ways that in return triggers the true beliefs of the inner self to become dysfunctional. Closed Systems deny the environment is about them, they refuse to accept the feedback from the environment, and they are very adept at even just ignoring the environment. A Closed System continues to become more dysfunctional within itself while continuing to blame the environment for its dysfunction. Closed Systems might feel safe and secure and they might even appear to be functioning from its own view still the process remains the same, they deny even that they are denying. A Closed System might not really lose anything, still a Closed System will not gain anything either.

It isn't easy having a loved one with an addiction nor is it easy being the addict. We are all human beings we all have frailties, sympathies, and many inconsistencies by our very nature of being human. "Natural man is an enemy of God". We all have similar internal systems, organs, program models and processes they operate by. The patterns and processes of the way the mind, emotions, behaviors, beliefs all develop, and function are the same just based on being human. We might all have different thought, emotion, behavior, and belief. Still, the nature of their development is the same from person to person. Even though a human being is the most intelligent creation we are aware of, the way in which the human brain functions works counter to our progression at times. Life's experience itself might cause a person to have anxiety of being around others. Some people lack confidence, some have a low self-esteem. Human beings not only misjudge others many misjudge themselves. Human beings by their very nature have inadequacies, weaknesses, fears, doubts, overwhelming or negative emotion. We don't understand things at times depending upon our life experience and the conscious perception of the experience. Human beings have the tendency to quickly just deny not only their behaviors even their thought and feelings. This denial can go to a point of convincing ourselves that we don't feel or think a certain way. These kind of programs and responses are a natural part of our human structure, patterns and processes. By our very nature we are an enemy of God and a danger to our own happiness and progression. Just having faith or even hope of a thing can bring an automatic response of doubt in self or another. So much of the nature of being human must be overcome in order for a human being to change, progress, even learn or feel happy.

A small part of the human brain is objective, this we refer to as the conscious. The conscious is the only part of the brain able to perceive, evaluate, judge or decide.

I struggle with just saying it like it is or beating around the bush, so I don't offend anyone. The fact of the matter is, there isn't time to beat around the bush. Addiction is destroying the addict, their families, the community, and this can go on for generations or it can stop. The choice is ours. Helping the addict can be hard enough itself, then there's the process of helping the family heal and overcome. The subconscious part of the human brain is not thinking it is only processing and storing data. The conscious part of the brain tells the subconscious what is perceived, evaluated, judged and decided about the data. The subconscious then processes that conscious data about the data and stores that with the data.

We are responsible for our own subconscious programs based upon the environment's we are in and our conscious opinions and decisions about our environment. If we have addictions, we are Closed Systems, if we have family members suffering from addictions, we are Closed Systems. A Closed System responds to the data and feedback in its environment by simply denying the feedback. A Closed System responds to the data and feedback in its environment by refusing to put up with the feedback. A Closed System responds to the data and feedback in its environment by just ignoring or diminishing the feedback to not be of any significance.

Generally speaking, all the family really desires is their loved one back. In the process, however, many things have been said and done which have caused a lot of pain. Pain doesn't just disappear on its own there is a process of overcoming our pain just as there is a process of overcoming an addiction. It takes a community to heal.

There are different components required in order to be an addict and remain an addict. An addict must be what is called a Closed System and it takes a Closed System to create an addiction. An Open System will not create addiction nor an addict. A Closed System is only capable of duplicating itself. An Open System is capable of continually working with its environment to overcome any system weaknesses, to develop any potential within itself. A Closed System is easy to be, they appear stable, they are predictable and there are few things a closed system will tolerate. Being predictable, simply means that when they are given feedback from their environment, they have a consistent way they respond to the feedback. A Closed System is an individual where you already know whether they are going to respond positive or negative to a situation. Their responses are so automatic that oftentimes other people in their environment won't even approach them anymore because they already know the closed system's response. A closed system does not grow, it thinks it is, but a closed system can gain nothing. An Open System is capable of overcoming anything and will learn and grow to understand all things in its environment. A closed system will even deny that it is closed. Things are traditional, standardized and whatever is going on in the environment will be denied, refused or repressed by the closed system. As a result of this many problems, in the closed systems surroundings never get addressed. This might be all good and well if it's just a plumbing problem. When it is a problem with a human being, the consequences of denying, refusing, or repressing the problem only adds fuel to the fire of the problem. An Open System admits, accepts and expresses regarding the plumbing and individual's problem. It isn't always easy to be open, we are not trained, raised nor programmed to be open. As innocent children we are born Open Systems. Our environment and everything in it fascinate us and gets our attention and after a period of time an infant will even begin to respond to the feedback in its environment. As we grow and become programmed by our care givers, our culture, society and others we gradually become closed systems. We become closed systems because our care givers are closed systems, our culture, society and others are closed systems. Again. What exactly is a closed system? A Closed System is a system that denies the information going on around it, it can be as simple as saying, "No, I didn't hear what you said", and then leaving it there. Denying can appear innocent though it is still the signs of a closed system. A closed system will refuse the information going on in its environment; this might become more emotional than just denying. Refusing might be as simple of a response as, "No I didn't hear what you said and frankly I'm not interested in your opinion." Repressing information going on in the environment might just involve an action to the information that might insinuate not really caring, something as simple as just walking away and ignoring. I know that no one is perfect, and I am not talking about being perfect, I am simply explaining Holographic Human Transformation Theory of an Open verses a Closed System. A Closed system can be easily created, and an Open system will not create a closed system. The fact is that an Open system be an environment where other systems are all able to grow, develop, and learn in.

I used to get spanked for misbehaving now as a parent you can get in trouble for physically discipline your child. I am not advocating spanking or speaking against it. I am only saying this, whatever the feedback going on in the environment is going on for good reason. In some schools in America even children take guns to school, a closed system chooses to deal with this by having police or security guards check or and carry guns.

This is closed system response. Deny, Refuse, Repress, this is refusing and an attempt to just repress the behavior. "No, my son wouldn't do that." "I'm not putting up with that I'll give teachers guns to protect themselves from their students." "Guns? Children carrying guns at school, I'm sure there's a good reason, they're not really going to hurt anyone." These are simple examples of a closed system response. The simple predictability of the closed system response becomes a resource for making the problems more extreme and closed system individuals involved finding more ways to manipulate the closed system. The closed system just continues further and further into being closed, predictable and not being able to truly recognize any real solutions to any problems. The closed system responds to the surface of the problem to just make it deny itself, respond angrily to intimidate it into not continuing and finally just justifies or minimizes the problem. This process makes the closed system feel strong and stable at first until it gets to the state of somehow justifying it. The closed system is a process of justifying and minimizing the systems own limiting beliefs instead of being open and willing to grow as a system and change in order to meet the change and needs of the individuals in its environment.

There are different systems, even in being human by our nature as individuals we are systems and then there are man-made systems as well. A family is a system; business is systems, nature itself is a system. Human beings as individuals come together in different systems like the family and society these are all systems. A system is defined as an interdependent group of items or individuals forming a unified whole. These groups interact under influences of related forces similar forces organized with established procedures. Systems have common purpose and naturally tend to a state of equilibrium. Systems by nature as a society or social system become stultifying or oppressive. Systems by nature are not closed, they become closed through systemic error. An error that is not determine by chance in the system but is introduced by an inaccuracy as observed or measurement inherent in the system itself.

A Closed System is an Addictive System and the greatest tragedy is that a Closed System is running from and trying to hide from the Undeniable, the Self, within the system. The problems within the system are indicators of problems (within) the system already has, as it has been existing and has established it to be. The denying, refusing, and repressing of the system itself is inaccurate, and the problem in the environment is inherent because of the system. As an individual, how often do we stand up and admit to our weaknesses, or accept we are able and ready to develop more? How often do we express progression in our behaviors? As a society, we don't admit many of the problems in our own communities, let alone accept that we could help and express with our behaviors ways of helping. Oftentimes, those that do admit, accept, and express are considered the sympathizer and indulgers, even considered unintelligent. This process becomes addicted to itself to its own principles, ideas, identity, and if this doesn't change, by the nature of the system needing to grow and always change the problems the closed system has to deal with just grow more intense. The natural process of seeking a state of equilibrium within the system; between the different parts of the system; performing 1 or more vital functions together. When any part of this system is denied, refused or repressed within the system the part becomes more and more apparent in the system to get the system to change. This will continue until the system completely burst inside out. Do you see yet the pattern of the addict, alcoholic, out of control child? The problem won't fix itself, the system won't fix it, society won't fix it, and our culture won't fix it. We must stop denying they are an addict or that they have a problem, and we have to admit that they have a problem. We must stop refusing to be aware of their needs and behaviors, we must accept that they do have needs and their behaviors are seeking to fill their needs. We must stop repressing their needs and behaviors; we must find ways to express to them other ways to fulfil their needs.

There are different Major Meta Programs required to be Closed Systems in order to maintain the addictive state. These Major Meta Programs consists of Memory, Time, Identity, Communication, Wisdom, Family, and Sin just to name a few. I will get into these in greater detail later on in this.

It takes a lot of effort to maintain the system as a Closed System. Most any and all Data and Feedback from the environment (outside of the system) must be Denied, Refused, and Repressed to keep the system closed. Over a period of time all the efforts involved to be able to Deny,

Refuse, and Repress any Data or Feedback consumes and controls all the thoughts, feelings, and behaviors of the Whole of the System until there seems to be no Whole (no Self) left within the system at all. The system literally becomes nothing more than the Personality, Identity, Internal communications, Emotions, Beliefs, Character traits, and Strategies just to support the Denial, the Refusal, and the Repressing of the Data and Feedback.

Change the locks on the doors more often. Get locks on doors to rooms inside the house, purchase safes to keep your guns and jewelry in. Are you beginning yet to see as a family or loved one of an addict that you become consumed with all the ridiculous ways to try to keep yourself from allowing the addicts behaviors to have any effect on you? No matter how much you do, no matter how often you cry yourself to sleep, no matter how many support groups you go to, the problem remains the same.

The addict is a closed system, the addict/alcoholic, whatever the addiction is too, the addict is great at denying, refusing, and repressing anything and everything you or anyone else tries to say to them. The addict's denial can be as simple as, "no I'm not using", "I used one time that's all". The refusal becomes angry where they are offended that you think they'd use. You hurt their feelings for accusing them. It's your fault they ever used. The repressing stage from the addict is where they just don't contact you anymore or don't come out of their room anymore and other avoidance behaviors just behaviors to make it seem invisible.

The lying, the anger, the excuses, other negative emotional responses, and justifications to the feedback begin to appear to be the individual as they state that the problem isn't theirs and blaming others for their problems are all symptoms of a Closed Addictive System. The more closed the person becomes the more they have to lie, become emotional and make excuses for their actions. All of their identity, personality, emotions and thoughts, their beliefs and behaviors take on the role of all the denials, refusals and repressing. The individual as they truly are seems to have disappeared, like they are not even in there anymore, though they are. It takes a closed system to create closed systems; you cannot be open to other beliefs, values and ideas and remain a closed system. When others have beliefs, values and ideas different from yours and it offends you or somehow hits you as wrong, you are a closed system. A closed system will close other systems around it and the whole family or whatever else the system might be will implode.

"Children reflect denied needs and repressed desires of parents and siblings". So, the addiction does not just come from a bottle or a pipe, the internet or a needle. Addiction begins with needs and desires. Sometimes, these needs and desires aren't even the addicts. This makes it hard for them to comprehend, let alone overcome. The more closed the system is the greater the addiction becomes. An example of the addiction being a response to the denied needs of a parent or other individual in the system is when a child has a serious illness and the parent might deny the severity of it. The child might state they are fine and deny their symptoms or amplify their symptoms and nothing seems to get rid of them. I have heard many stories from people in recovery who had medical problems in their childhood and became the comfort and support to get the parent through. We can all understand these kinds of experiences, life can be difficult and oftentimes we put a smile on or isolate, either response is a closed system response. Denying our own needs, repressing and refusing to get help for yourself. The child or other individual take on these denied desires and needs but don't understand them and just respond closed themselves. In other words, they do things to deny, refuse and repress all they feel from the needs and desires of the parent or system. I have heard it said that light always overcomes the dark. A Closed System lives in the dark and will deny the light, refuse to accept light when it is offered and repress the light if it does get in, with even more darkness.

Addiction is hard to overcome but it is not impossible. Again, one person does not an addict alcoholic make. It took a team to get them here and it takes a team to get them out and a community to help keep them out.

We live in a closed society and grew up with closed families in closed environments. When we are young and innocent, we can imagine and believe as we just do, though it's been the exception for decades that creative children were allowed to continue in their journey. These creative children when given the boundaries to imagine, dream and desire become today's talents and leaders. Boundaries are important but not to the point of closing out another's beliefs. Only a closed system fears another's beliefs, their dreams and desires. We all grow up, but what we become when we do grow up is greatly affected by whether others around us are open or closed systems.

A Closed System is very predictable. A Closed System is not going to change on its own, it may change with the natural forces of life, but a Closed System is not choosing to change. Closed Systems will also often times deny that they are closed. The more the system is closed, the greater the forces come to attempt to open the system. These greater forces to attempt to open the system are feedback to the closed system attempting for force it to stop denying. When you already know the way a person or other system is going to respond to you, that system is predictable, therefore, the system is closed.

Being a Closed System is a natural state for human beings, being closed is about our boundaries, which we also wrongly perceive as our values and beliefs. Being a Closed System has nothing to do with our values and our beliefs. Quite the contrary, the boundaries of a Closed System are in complete denial of our true values and beliefs. Our boundaries are only regarding the knowing of what is truly going on in our environment. Boundaries keep feedback out or let the feedback in. Boundaries are around us not within us being. Just because we disagree or disapprove should not determine whether or not we are aware it is going on. When we even deny it is happening, we cannot evaluate, judge or decide about it. We came here to experience this life and to grow and learn to live the Gospel here. How do we learn, let alone grow when we deny things are happening? When we judge what is happening as we acknowledge that it is.

The whole purpose of the Closed System is to keep the system from having to acknowledge its true beliefs and values. Closed Systems have become very acceptable in today's society, to a point of an Open System seeming to be without boundaries or knowledge. When the fact is an Open System does have boundaries and is very knowledgeable. Closed Systems just keep doing the same thing over and over again thinking it is moving forward.

The Closed System is referred to as an Addictive System based upon its inability to admit its environmental data and feedback because of its boundaries. It can almost take a disaster for a Closed System, in order to let its boundaries down and recognize what is truly going on around it. The environment and all we notice consciously from it serves the purpose of opening our inner self. The things we see and hear; all we are aware of that is happening around us serves the purpose of getting our inner self to grow, and to change.

In a Closed, Addictive System, the inner self refuses to change, it will go to any length to make sure that the environmental feedback (perception) isn't about the inner self to the point of displaying more and more self-defeating dysfunctional patterns to try to make the feedback go away and leave the inner self alone. The feedback will not go away, the more the addicted closed systems tries to deny, refuse, and repress the feedback, the more the feedback increases in occurrence and intensity. The more frequent and intense the feedback from the environment becomes, the more dysfunctional the "inner self" thoughts, emotional, and behavioral patterns become. All of this just serves to keep making the problem worse and worse, seemingly without end, to a point of giving up all hope. This is often times where the addictive system loses family, friends, a job, and sometimes everything.

Life seems hopeless at this point for all parties dealing with the closed addicted system. Being a Closed System can feel safe and comfortable at first but as individuals, continuing on this closed path may lead even to loss of life.

A Closed System becomes addicted to whatever thoughts, emotions, behaviors, and substances it takes to keep the feedback from its environment out of its boundaries. The addiction becomes a result of attempting to protect the inner self, not the environment or how we interact with it but our views, beliefs and perceptions of our self. This is one of the reasons the addict becomes selfish and seems to not care about people, places and things around it. Addiction is defined as a habitual compulsive need to habit forming substances. Addiction is characterized by tolerance and by well-defined psychological symptoms upon withdrawal. Being addicted to anything is the natural progression of being a closed system. The way the addict views his or herself, must be denied, refused and repressed by their boundaries and limitations. The addict's true beliefs and true perceptions of the self, have to be denied in order for all the addict behaviors to continue, and the addict behaviors continue for this purpose. They will seemingly go to any means to avoid having to admit, accept and express all they truly are or view themselves to be. The addict is not happy with their addict behaviors, these behaviors are a shield, so they don't have to face their true self.

Chapter 2

CLOSED SYSTEM'S BOUNDARIES ARE NOT FLEXIBLE/PERMEABLE

An Open System Admits, Accepts and Expresses all Data and Feedback from its environment. Yes, even Data and Feedback from a Closed System. I know this is not an easy task. At the same time, I know it does work.

Overcoming Addiction takes strength, knowledge and wisdom from others involved with the addict. Both the addict and others working to help the addict must work to maintain or become an Open System. Whether the system is the family, community, a church or a treatment facility, they must be Open themselves to Admitting, Accepting and Expressing to assist the addict. Fighting a Closed System on its own terms only serves to strengthen the boundaries and limitations which support the Closed System. Fighting a Closed System can also tempt an Open System to become closed, thus the saying "What we resist, persists". When something is in our life consistently and we think fighting it will make it go away, we just become more closed to the options and abilities within ourselves to overcome the obstacle. Life has ups and downs. Life has obstacles regardless of our own efforts, knowledge and choice. Whatever your life experience might be, the feedback in your environment means something of significance to you and the feedback is significant. Every system has built in inadequacies, problems, and potential; systems by nature grow and change with experience. Man use to live in caves and go to hunt and pick each meal, the system changed to the way it is today. Today's system should continue to change based upon feedback within the system itself.

Problems, obstacles, challenges are indicators of greater potential within a given system when we try to resist the challenge the challenge becomes more intense.

Being and remaining an Open System means that whatever the addict says, feels and does, is admitted, accepted and expressed in an Open System. Admitted merely means here the acknowledgment, perception, actually seeing and hearing what the addict says, how the addict feels and what the addict does. The opposite of admitting is denying and denying would mean saying "no, they did not say and do that, I never saw nor heard that, I don't know what we can do to help." This is a common response in families; the addict finally gets arrested or in some kind of trouble due to the addiction, and the family wonders why they didn't see it coming. The family, the system whatever the system is also is working to protect its inner view of self. No individual is perfect yet, and no system is a perfect system. Still, we all could learn and grow. We all can look back and recognize the signs and symptoms, they were obvious all along. Hindsight reflects a closed system. An open system will observe the signs and symptoms as they appear, they will begin to dialogue about what they have observed. An open system will theorize from their observations and dialogues and will implement their theories and continue to observe and dialogue all along the course. In very simple terms, this is a first step in admitting verses denying. This is merely a process of observing the feedback, the addict behavior, the seemingly obstacles of and within the system. Just observe first and foremost.

Accept merely means that the acknowledgment of it is dialogued internally within an Open System itself (you) and New Theories of what it might mean and what might be the best approach to dealing with it followed with discussion of this with the Closed System; the addict or obstacle. The acceptance aspect of the open system is the discovery process of the potential within the system that the system has prior tried to ignore, indulge or justify. Discovering the meaning of the environmental feedback to the system itself. What does the feedback indicate about the system? How does the feedback relate to the way the system is today and has the system had any intuitions regarding this feedback when it comes up? What action within the system might the feedback indicate the system look at for any system weaknesses and potential for greater growth within and for the system? Systemic error: Is not happen stance just in the environment, it is inherent in the system itself, and it is observable and measurable. Every system has good and bad, right and wrong, strength and weakness. No system is perfect. Any addict behavior is a result of systemic errors being denied, refused, and repressed by the very system they are a part of. The open system knows this and looks at itself to theorize what it might be attempting to avoid about its true self. Just dialogue about the environment feedback, create sentences that are non-judgmental and observable; measurable descriptions of the feedback and the system. Then theorize what strengths the system may have and what weaknesses the system might have that this addict feedback is a result of, and what the system might do to address the real issue of itself. The real view of itself, the whole family, school, community, attempting to avoid its own unavoidable, and its true identity. The systems true view of itself, the systems true beliefs, and the true purpose of the system in the first place. The true potential already in the system that perhaps the system hadn't identified yet.

Expressed is merely the consistent repeated doing of the "what might be the best" approach to dealing with what was acknowledged, perceived, dialogued. and theorized. Implementing the new theories of the systems true views, beliefs, purpose and watching the environmental feedback. This process continues in an open system, observing, dialoging, theorizing, and implementing. Observe the feedback from this process, dialogue and theorize, implement, and start again at observing the feedback. It is a continual process of going through cycles if you are dealing with a closed system. A closed system however is a process of deny, I didn't even know, refuse, just responding by not accepting the fact that it's about the system and then repress it just brush it away somehow. Repeat, repeat, repeat. As this process continues, the Open Systems continues to be Open to more Data and Feedback from the Closed System (the addict) repeating this same process over and over. Acknowledging, perceiving, seeing, hearing, internally dialoging with self, contemplating more New Theories and Expressing the knowledge gained through dealing with the Closed System.

Having the family, the community, whom ever is involved with the addict a part of this process, is vital to the success of overcoming the Closed System. When others involved with the addict are at odds with one another the closed system will win.

This is a process and takes effort of everyone's behalf and it is possible to accomplish. Everyone must be involved and as the saying goes, "on the same page."

From your dialogue of more and better approaches to deal and sharing this with the addict, then repeating these possible approaches while continuing to take in Data and Feedback and repeat the Open System process. This is a simple description of an Open System. Being open is not an easy process especially coming from a world where boundaries and barriers are just an expected part of our lives.

This does not mean that you have no boundaries in dealing with the closed system; it simply means that your open system boundaries are permeable and flexible. In other words, you hear what they say and see what they do as well as the other Data coming from them. Having been consciously aware of what they are sharing you simply process this data yourself. You are welcome to discuss the data with another person, though please do so with someone who is an Open system. Discussing or internally dialoguing or writing in a journal your information and new theories of ways of doing things with the closed system can be vital to your progress, as well as the closed system's progress.

The expressing is simply the plans and strategies implemented of your new theories for responding based upon your own perception, evaluation, judgment, and decision. Sound draining? It's really quite easily done and very efficient when repeated over a period of time. Light will overcome the dark, though the light cannot become dim because of the dark. The light cannot be denied, even in the dark. How many of us have become less light due to our own denial, refusal and repressing of another Closed System's responses. Addiction cannot be denied, refused, or repressed. A

Closed System is an Addictive system and can only duplicate itself, making more Closed Systems.

The good news is that the greater (or worse) the Data and Feedback trying to come into the Closed System which the Closed Systems Denies, Refuses, and Represses, the Greater (or better) the potential within the Closed System is trying to avoid. In other words, Greater the Self-potential. The more you are willing to say, to show, and to do at the Closed System, the greater the potential within that systems potential that the Closed Systems has been trying to avoid. You have felt battered at before, the environment seemingly tormenting you, and at some time it dawned on you that something within you needed what the battering was about.

Remember, the Open System Admits the Data and Feedback, yes, even from the Closed System. It Admits, Accepts and Expresses it back to the Closed System. Sounding simpler yet?

I have a sense that you already knew this. It is not necessarily just man's wisdom, the scriptures reference that God will give us nothing that we cannot overcome, and He says, "Come unto me and I will show unto you your weaknesses". He will turn our weaknesses into strengths.

To educate means to "Draw out". This is what truly happens when the addict truly heals their dysfunctional programs and becomes an Open System. What has been inside of them, the whole time finally begins to grow and shine from them. This is also all that many families and loved ones are seeking from the experience, just to have their loved one back. When the system becomes open to the dysfunction in its environment and addresses it by turning any potential weakness into potential strength, the whole system becomes open again. The whole system continues to be educated, to have the true potential of not only view, but also true beliefs and strengths. There is nothing to be closed to or about, the system understands it has continual potential built into it to grow.

Education is ongoing and progressive. We are all here to gain education, we are here to "Draw out" all of our potential and become it. D&C 130 18-19; "Whatever principle of intelligence we attain unto in this life, it will rise with us in the resurrection. And if a person gains more knowledge and intelligence in this life through his diligence and obedience than another, he will have so much the advantage in the world to come." Proverbs 24, 5 "A wise man is strong; yea a man of knowledge increaseth strength."

WHAT IS THE CURE FOR ADDICTION?

What is the cure for addiction?
Abstinence.
How does one abstain?
Stop.
What causes addictions?
Attempts to avoid the unavoidable.
What in life is unavoidable?
Self.
Why would one attempt to avoid themselves?
Because of their shame, guilt or fear.
What causes shame, guilt and fear?
Not being all we are able to be.
Why aren't we being all we are able to be?
Because we deny, refuse and repress that we can.
What is the cure for our denial and such? Believe. Janey Marvin

OPEN VERSES CLOSED SYSTEM EVALUATION

Take the following test and score out your answers to determine the areas you might be Closed or Open in. This is the beginning to finding your way out of your addictive patterns.

SCALE TO CALIBRATE YOUR SYSTEM

1) How much time do you spend each week organizing for or because of others? (do not count job time).

   a. 10 mins. _____, b. ½ hr. _____, c. 1 hr. _____. d. 2 hrs. _____ e. more_____

2) Rate yourself in the role of the family organization.

1._____, 2. _____, 3. _____, 4. _____

3) Rate yourself in the stability of your family.

1._____, 2. _____, 3. _____, 4. _____

4) Rate your family's abilities to Self-organize.

1._____, 2. _____, 3. _____, 4. _____

5) Most of your free time is spent:

1. Doing the same thing.
2. Doing 3 different things
3. Doing 7 different things
4. Doing a multitude of different things

6) When something upsets you, you…

1. Take action then
2. Let others take action
3. Gather information and opinions of others
4. No action

7) All around stability is a good thing in a family.

1. Yes
2. No
3. Sometimes

8) Rate yourself on the way you deal with chaos. 1 to 4 with 4 being highest.

1._____, 2. _____, 3. _____, 4. _____

9) Which part of the airplane is the part that makes it fly?

A. Engine
B. Wings
C. Body
D. All of the above

10) How many denied needs and desires do you think you have?

1. None
2. 1 to 3
3. 4-7
4. More

11) Do you spend most of your time focused on the:

A. Past
B. Present
C. Future
D. None of the above

Score your answers: Add any "1"'s separately. Add all other numbers together for a whole score.

1. (1-2-3-4-5)
2. (1-2-4-5)
3. (1-3-4-5)
4. (5-3-2-1)
5. (5-4-2-1)
6. (2-3-1-5)
7. (5-1-3)
8. (5-3-2-1)
9. (3-4-2-1)
10. (5-3-4-1)
11. (5-3-4-1)

Scoring your Open vs. Closed System

If your score was:

1-11 = Excellent: You are a very rare human being; you are an Open System. You have great knowledge and wisdom. You can discern many things about yourself and others. You have access to your own knowing which may at times surprise even you how easily it just comes to your mind. Each experience you have is a learning experience for you and you having discovered that the more you learn the more there is to learn. You have a multitude of options of dealing with life's problems and often find that you are already prepared for them even before they come. Disorder in your life is discontinuous because your personal wisdom and knowledge just grows automatically.

12-27 = Good: You are Closed in primary areas of your life; this is because of things from your past you still don't trust your own judgment about yet. You still have hurts from others which you blame yourself for. You have the strengths within to grow from these hurts to a point of even being an example of strength to others. You work to have your dreams and care for your own needs and get discouraged, feeling drained doing so. You handle chaos and disorder well though you will not do anything to nurture yourself afterwards. You struggle in general with nurturing yourself. You know yourself and are able to discern things in others; you just have a difficult time expressing this in your actions.

28-42 = Fair: You are functioning at ½ of your ability. On the verge of giving up and struggling with that because you truly want to keep moving forward. Sometimes, it seems you don't really know who you are anymore, but you keep hoping. What you hear and perceive is about ½ of what is available as are your expressions in return. You experience feeling misunderstood and not important enough at times. You have physical symptoms of these experiences, though mild, you rarely express this. You have memories of hurts from your past and fear they will be repeated in your future. You blame "Either" you or others for your struggles only find answers about half the time. You greatest challenge is to believe in yourself and find others who believe in you. You are using only .50 of what is inside you, at your full potential you may be 2X's all you are today.

43-55 = Poor: You are a Closed System and do not see that you are. You blame others for most of your problems. You are an Addict. Whether your addiction is to a substance, life patterns or of a non-tangible bases, you are addicted. Your thoughts, feelings and behaviors are predictable because they are habitual, because you don't change. You are not even you anymore. You have become the Identity, Personality, thoughts, emotions and behaviors which do nothing for you except keep you addicted. (Closed). If you are going to begin to heal you will have to recognize what's going on inside of you. Recognize what you are doing and stop allowing yourself to continue to blame others. You will have to find Open Systems to be around as it is very difficult to become Open when you are surrounded by Closed Systems. Your system went into decline many years ago and you nor anyone else did anything to stop it. You can stop it. It won't be easy. You will go through times of chaos and disorder.

CHAPTER 3

LOST DESIRES, DREAMS, AND GOALS

A Closed System's Boundaries are not flexible nor permeable

Closed systems are not negotiable, the lines are drawn and its simple just don't cross the line or the consequences are to be ignored, retaliated at, or simply disregarded or justified away. Closed system's respond negatively to their environments feedback.

Addicted means to devote or surrender oneself, to something habitually or obsessively. In other words, to be addicted means to commit by a solemn act, often times by compelling motives and attachment to an objective. The habit is the prevailing disposition or character of a person's thoughts, feelings, and behaviors. Our thoughts, feelings, and behaviors are committed by solemn act and compelling motives and attachment to the object we are addicted to. We can be addicted to anything from substances to thoughts, feelings, and behaviors. The addiction can be to anything. The reason behind the addiction is to avoid the unavoidable, the true self. Nothing else really matters. Not others, not the self. Addiction is like cancer, and like cancer, cancer can kill the addict.

What are the compelling motives and the objective of the addiction? The addict didn't just wake up one day and become an addict. The compelling motive is to avoid the unavoidable, the true self. The source of the addiction has gained confidence from the rest of the system, convincing the system that it can take the pains and sufferings away. It doesn't matter if the addiction is to a substance or to just thinking patterns; these sources of the addiction have still convinced the system that it can fix the systems problems. The true self does not need to be acknowledged at all, as long as the addiction is used to avoid it.

We are all so much more than we generally acknowledge to be. We each have an inner-sense of right and wrong. We came into this life with great knowledge from the life we came here from. This knowledge is a real part of our being and we all have had a sense or an idea of these knowing's. All our prior knowledge added to all our knowledge and potential in this life gives us all the ability to be genius, limitless potential beings. As a Closed system, we will never reach our true potential.

Addiction is a compulsive need for and use of a behavior or habit-forming substance characterized by tolerance and by well-defined physiological symptoms upon withdrawal. Physiological symptoms are not only experienced from withdrawal from a substance, they are experienced when quitting behaviors or emotional responses and thought patterns.

What is the definition of tolerance? Tolerance is a capacity to endure pain or hardship, so these things do not decrease the addictive behaviors. Tough love will not drive the addict to quit the addictive behaviors. The truth is that tough love is addictive behavior from a Closed system. As the loved ones impose their concept or man's concept of tough love they need more and tougher love to endure the pain and hardship of the consequences of their own tough love approach. Consequences, whether natural or imposed upon the addict, creates a compelling need for more substance and addictive behaviors. This process of tolerance serves to increase denying, refusing, and repressing from the addict and the other closed systems "working" with the addict. Confronting angrily, punishing, living on the streets, whatever is being done to the addict that causes them pain or creates hardships for them only serves to increase their capacity to endure the pain and hardship leaving them more trusting in the addiction. Tolerance creates sympathies and indulgence for beliefs or practices differing from or conflicting with the true self, the unavoidable self. This increase of tolerance creates and increases their ability to sympathize and indulge the beliefs and practices in the addictive behaviors they have. This same process is happening with the closed systems imposing consequences on the addict. They then, become more trusting in their tough love approaches. Their beliefs and behaviors that are contrary to their true self. The greater the pain and hardship the more they need the addictive behaviors. Avoid, Avoid, Avoid, becomes the tolerated, trusted answer; believing in all the things they have to do to keep from having to face their true inner self. The part of themselves that does care for the family, the part that knows all the wrong they've done and hate themselves for. This is what the addict, whatever addicted to, faces when they stop using the substances or stop doing the addict behaviors. This applies to any closed system; the family or community closed system will begin to go through tolerance. Tolerance is a capacity of enduring pain and suffering and becoming less responsive to dysfunctional behaviors or substances through repeated use and exposure to it. Tolerance is the beginning of a Closed system; tolerance is the beginning of any addiction and any system adept at tolerance will create other systems adept at tolerance. Enduring Pain and Suffering to a point of not even responding to it. Again, did you truly think they used because they had free choice to do so? Did you think it brought them joy? Did you think it was vengeance? The more pain and suffering put upon them, the more they trust whatever the addiction is to because it helps them endure the pain and the suffering. You cannot humiliate them into change.

Tolerance indicates an ability to "endure" pain and suffering. This is a skill addicts have, a quality and competence of deferring great sufferings. It is a natural aptitude or becomes acquired by them through its nature. They become very skillful master at accomplishing this. Even when they overdose or become incarcerated, they often times do face some of the pain and suffering they went through and the pain and suffering they imposed upon others. Unless they take the proper steps and receive the right help from an Open system, they just return back to the addictive self again. Most anything seeking to help them face their true inner being, will be something they will fight at until they realize, they are only fighting themselves.

Pain or suffering can continue and increase without the addict ever giving in. Tolerance means they'll remain firm in their addiction under great suffering or intense pain without yielding due to the pain. Tolerance creates an association or relationship between the pain and suffering and whatever the addiction is to. There is a unity or harmony in action and effect between the pain and the addiction. The addict's thoughts and feelings function in accord with the pain and suffering. There becomes a forgiving nature, a state or habit of thoughts and feelings, even confidence in the thoughts and feelings supporting the addiction. Regardless of how opposing, or how antagonistic these might be to the persons true beliefs, the indulgence and sympathies built on this tolerance is completely incompatible with their true self. The self with the inner sense of right and wrong, the self with the knowledge from their prior existence, and from all their experiences in this life. All they seem to indulge and sympathize with in order to tolerate all the pain and suffering from the past, and all the pain and suffering through the addiction is incompatible with their true self.

Peace of mind is the opposite of both pain and suffering.

Their true self knows it is denied and becomes more and more dysfunctional, continually cycling through its dysfunctional patterns causing the self and others more pain and suffering. This is the unavoidable. There is no denying, refusing, nor repressing our true self. There is no running, hiding, avoiding the true self. Wherever we go, whatever we do, we will still always be what we truly are. What we truly are knows itself, it is all we have ever been and all we may ever be, and it is always you. The closed system process of avoiding the unavoidable makes a sense of greater confidence in the source of the addiction. Around and around and around it goes with other closed systems attempting to make it stop or just go away.

When progress is made in overcoming the addiction, the true self begins to awaken. The addict sees the conflicts and contradictions of their thoughts and feelings. The pain and suffering to themselves and others is automatically triggering more pain and suffering, and the addictive tolerance seeks to fix this again.

What happens with an addiction regarding tolerance is it takes more and more of the behaviors and or substances because of "tolerance", to get the same response to ease the compelling motives regarding the pains and sufferings of the addiction. The objective of the addiction isn't the substance, it is the responsive feeling of escape from the true self. The self never goes away in this life or in the life to come, and the addiction isn't the answer to the hatred and humiliation of self.

Peace of mind is the opposite of both pain and suffering.

Did you really think they did this because they enjoyed it?

Endurance, fortitude, stamina!!! Tolerance consists of sympathies or indulgences for beliefs or practices differing from or conflicting with one's own beliefs or practices. Everything the addict does to maintain the addiction is in conflict with the addict's beliefs and abilities. This internal response creates the tolerance effect. What? I thought the addict had tolerance and used more because they believed in it and loved the practice of their addiction. This isn't to elude that the drug itself adds to the tolerance system, though the individual themselves are the greater part of this process. There does reach a point with any addiction where the "high" no longer occurs, all it becomes about is survival.

The opposite of a relapse is to reform. Each reform must be based upon a greater improved condition. An increase or amended state of improvement by removing even more faults, more pains, and more sufferings. There must be on-going change for the better. The addict must learn to deal with ongoing pain and sufferings. The pain and suffering that can be triggered by a certain time of year, seeing a certain person, and etc.... The addict true self is very contrary to the dysfunctional person they seem to become during the addiction. The addict must remember the true self, must forgive self and others, and must learn ways to nurture the true self. The addict and any closed system must find peace of mind through all of life's struggles.

A Closed System is an Addictive System. There are many types of Addictions and any Closed System becomes Addicted to something. We are all Closed Systems; to some degree we all have addictions of some kind. There are three levels to being human; Mental, Emotional, and

Physical, and addictions occur on any and all levels. Addictions on a Mental level may appear as seemingly innocent thought patterns and perceptions with strong opinions. These thought patterns can become very harmful, even destructive to self and others. Addictions on an Emotional level are habitual emotional responses which can also harm the self and others. Physical level addictions are the most obvious and judged by others. These addictions are behavioral and substance addictions. Addictions on this level can be illegal and even cause death. We are Closed Systems and we all are addicted on some level to some habitual pattern, seeking some response attempting to avoid the unavoidable, the self. Attempting to avoid life's pains and suffering, whether we have been the victim, or the perpetrator is never the answer to life's problems.

We weren't born closed. Me came into this life innocent, and it has been our life experience, or at least our view of our life experience that's turned us into Closed Systems. Our childhood dreams disappeared, our great imaginations became realities that failed, and life as it might have been, seemed to have passed us by. So not true. That is another illusion. You are not lost; your reality is your imaginations and your life is waiting for your directions. You cannot go where you don't believe you can go. You cannot do what you don't believe you can do. You cannot know the path unknown to you until you experience it and gain knowledge from it. Parts of you might be missing your acknowledgment of them, and you might ask, "How can I acknowledge what I do not yet know?" It's really quite simple… Go to before its beginning. Where have you come from, before you became closed? Maybe you have to go to before you came to earth. What is your purpose here on earth? There are many references both in religion and in science as to the fact that everything needed for the success of a thing already exists about the thing before the thing ever began. Nothing has a beginning unless its potential already existed in its true form. Knowing or observing the something while it is still nothing is a strength some people have today.

Look at the people you care about and those who care about you ask them what potential they observe in you and share with them the potential you see in them. This is common human nature though it may be easier to do as the observer than as the observed.

Before you were born, you already had true potential to succeed at any and all of life's challenges. No life challenge would come to you without you having the potential to overcome it. This is just a simple fact as well as spiritual and scientific realities.

Look at those around you who are struggling with addictions and remember the potential you knew they once had. It didn't just go away; it is the True Self, and the True Self doesn't just disappear. The individual's Self View of their True Self limits the True Self from being all it already was able to be before it ever began.

Go back to before the beginning for your source of strength, hope, faith and direction.

A Closed system becomes nothing more than the very boundaries and limitation created to keep the System Closed. It takes lies, deceit, dishonesty, and many other thoughts, feelings, and behaviors to keep a System a Closed System. These very thoughts, feelings, and behaviors of the closed system are in conflict and are even contrary to the true self beliefs. The actual Identity of the Individual seems to just vanish and all that appears to be left of them are the foundations of the Addiction.

Our ability toward "Oneness", to be "One" with ourselves, our families, and society is gone when this happens. Our psychological identification is established just based upon the limits, boundaries, and inadequacies of the problems. We appear to Be Liars, Deceivers, Thieves, Selfish, and our Whole Identity seems to have become the thoughts, feelings, and behaviors that help tolerate the addiction. The addiction, whose sole purpose has been to keep us from having to face and to overcome ourselves.

Identity has burst! We are no longer ourselves. We only have access to the thoughts, emotions, and behaviors of our devotion to the Addiction. This is in an effort to attaining a goal with a true objective buried deep within us.

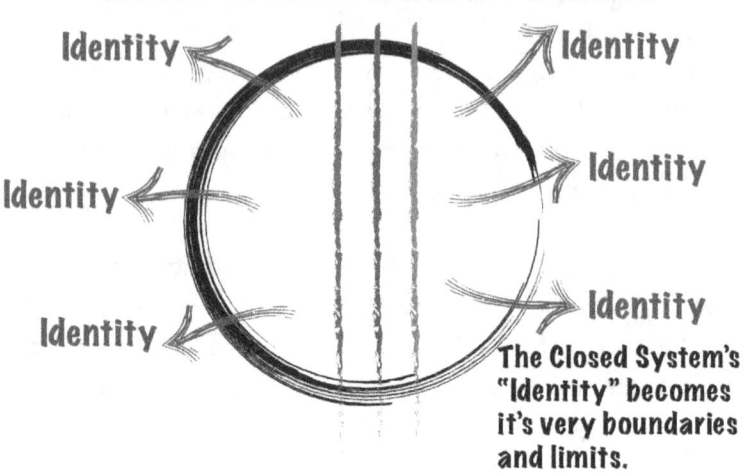

The compulsive drive for more and more of the substance or behaviors is because these very things differ and are in conflict with the addict's own beliefs and practices of the ways to attain the goal and achieve the objective: Tolerating with self-sympathy, while indulging false beliefs and practices that differ from and conflict with their own beliefs and practices. Each time they allow the addiction to win, their own conflicting beliefs, practices, goals, and objectives need more and more of the substance or behavior in an effort to avoid the unavoidable self. Their own beliefs and practices, their own true knowing of their own goals and objectives gets sicker and sicker inside of them. They appear to have disappeared and all they see is through the boundaries of the addiction. They cannot live with themselves anymore; they have to remove themselves as much as possible by whatever means it might take. Life for them has become unbearable. Not because of their addiction but because they do know what they truly believe, they do know what they wanted to accomplish in their life, they do know the way they'd like to be, and that they have a purpose.

They can never run fast enough or far enough because they are running from themselves. Not just things they have experienced, also, things they truly believe in and have inside of them and are able to put into practice.

They truly are not themselves anymore and the addiction deceives them into believing in it instead of them. Without the addiction, they long to overcome their own fears and shame and guilt.

They must deceive themselves into having sympathy and indulging in beliefs and practices which are truly different or in conflict with their True Self, their potential self. In fact, the whole purpose of the addiction is to create the illusion of the Self-View to keep the True Self captive.

YOU DON'T EVEN KNOW – by Janey Marvin

You don't even know who you are anymore, and you don't even think that we care. You think we see you thru the eyes of addiction, We see you through the eyes of our prayers. You believe you've become the lies you tell, to others and even yourself. The deceit it takes to keep the addiction, the depths on Earth to reach your man-made hell. You run around both day and night feeling lost and alone, there's nothing else anyone can say to convince you, you're not home. We remember who you are and know who you can be. The lie is not within you; deceits not filled your soul.

Surrounded in your prison, trapped and feeling cold. There is no place where you can run, no place where you can hide, to escape the way we love you, the you we know inside. How deep must you go, how cold must you be, before your eyes are opened, before you're ready to see? You are not destined nor are you alone. We're all in this together, none is on their own.

God placed us here on Earth, none were sent to lose. Put down the drug, the lies and hate, put down the pills and booze. You aren't what the devil wants you to think. It's not that hard or far to turn your life around, your brothers and sisters abound. No matter what has happened or how far you go, it's never too late. You're in our prayers, you're in our hearts, we'll meet you at the gate.

I don't know if this helps you feel better or worse, I do know this is the truth. I have a saying, "I'd rather hear the ugly truth than a beautiful lie, any day."

ASSIGNMENT: DO THE SENSORY PERSONALITY PROFILE

Personality Questionnaire

REFERENCES

1) When noticing my own topics of thought or conversation, my greatest area of focus is:

A. Things I've seen then heard
B. Things I've heard then seen
C. Things I've done
D. Things I relate with
E. Process of doing things
F. The end results

2) In my opinion the primary facts may be found thru the following questions?

A. Why
B. What
C. Which
D. Who
E. How
F. Where
G. When

3) The most useful elements (aspects) in life are:

A. Reason, Ideas
B. Meaning, Values
C. Actions, Intuitions
D. Relationships
E. How
F. Strategies
G. Time/Self

4) Action should be based upon

A. Reason
B. Meaning
C. Intuition
D. Relationships
E. Planning
F. Status

5) 5) The greatest connection for me is in the:

A. Past
B. Present
C. Future

Regarding:

A. Things seen
B. Things heard
C. Actions taken
D. Relationships
E. Function of
F. Skills

6) The one thing always being focus of any matter for me is:

A. Concept
B. Value
C. Intuition
D. Association
E. Qualities
F. Means to and end

7) The most important indication for myself is:

A. Why
B. What
C. Which
D. Who
E. How
F. Where
G. When

DECISIONS

1) The most important action process of deciding for me is:

A. Power
B. Method
C. Ideas
D. Character
E. Value
F. Actions

2) A thing is beyond question to me based upon:

A. Relating
B. Action
C. Representation
D. Thought
E. Cognition
F. Natural logic

3) When given alternatives, I make my choice based on:

A. Circumstances
B. The people
C. Design
D. Conditions

E. Insight
F. Moral principle

4) When I explain my conclusions of a thing I emphasize:

A. Personal relation
B. Mutual interests
C. Past concepts
D. Personal ideas
E. Subjective intuitions
F. Objective intuitions

5) Good choice requires:

A. Strategies and their relations
B. Good communication in relationships
C. Reason and character
D. Belief and ideas
E. Action for others and meaning
F. Past value and present action

MOTIVATORS

1) My driving power comes from:

A. Present action and my personal character
B. Future purpose and present intuitions
C. Tomorrows advantage, yesterday's principles
D. Yesterday's moral values and tomorrows plan
E. Ways I have viewed the world its meaning
F. My ancestors and my future knowledge

2) I am most easily excited by:

A. My intuitions of the world and the this relates
B. The character of others and their actions
C. Created steps for the world for its future based upon the past
D. Being able to know ways to make my life change
E. Personal relations helping me bridge my own past
F. Having relationships today with people I can create ideas with

3) My greatest motive of success is based upon:

A. Action of others and intuition if they pertain to the future
B. My view of character and my own present actions
C. C. Great meaning/value from what I hear and knowing the end result
D. Strategies in self for the future with meaning from the past
E. Others relating to it and the idea already existing
F. Good reasons and personally relating to them

4) I most often help others to action by:

A. By sharing my enthusiasm and future beliefs in them
B. My data and actions with value to them
C. Research into the past and strategies of the future
D. My knowledge and data I got it from
E. Introducing them to people I know to share their ideas
F. Helping them find reasons relate to them

5) When given options I'd prefer to:

A. Act on intuition and self-character
B. Know future processes and question the present.
C. Have all my data around me and decide my functions
D. Plan my future based on what I have gathered.
E. Know its relationship now to visions of my past.
F. Perceive the representation in all things and their relating.

6) In most areas of my life, I empower others with:

A. My own intuitions and help with my personal traits
B. Example of character and my actions
C. Reinforcing their value and my knowledge to attain
D. My experience in the area and words of wisdom
E. Relate with them well and share my imaginative visions
F. Worldly reason for their personal empowerment

7) As long as I have the following, I can keep going:

A. Building my action and intuition with good belief in my character
B. Focus on the future and emotional intuitions with my taking little to no action.
C. Meaning and detailed instruction
D. Future goals and good ethics
E. Relationships with others and good reason.
F. Imaginative ideas that I feel connected to.

PERSONALITY PROFILE EVALUATION RESULTS

In the section marked References count the number of A, B, C, D, E, F. The letters you have the most of are indicating your Reference senses. We each have two Reference, two Decision and two Motivator senses, remembering that we also have sensory blocks, and these may be indicated by a general firing order with none or a minimum of a sense indicated in the firing order. The letters indicating References of letters A and B together and C and D together and E and F together will indicate one of two Primary sensory firing order personalities you may have. These senses will be the first and the fourth sense fired in the firing order.

From this point, in the section marked Decisions count the number of A, B, C, D, E, F. The letters you have the most of here will indicate the second and fifth sense fired in your sensory personality firing order.

Count the number of letters in the section marked as Motivators and the majority of the letters and indicated senses here will identify your third and sixth sense fired in your sensory personality firing order.

Beginning with your reference senses, going to your decision then motivator senses find your closest sensory firing order from the list of different personality firing orders listed below.

Determine your most aligned firing order remembering that we all have sensory blocks and these sensory blocks will also be indicated in this questionnaire. The sensory blocks are identified based upon fewer or zero sense answers in the Reference, Decisions, and Motivator sections and in the most similar firing order identified.

Whenever there is a sensory block, if the central nervous system can fire through the block the next sense fired processes the blocked sense information based upon its own functions which then puts that sense on overload and gives a very different perspective to the blocked sensory functions.

Answers A and B, then C and D, then E and F are similar in subconscious function. Any G answer indicates a reference to focus on time instead of self.

Identify you major Personality Profile and read the description. There is endless information we can place in these descriptions such as Elements, body organs, and disease. Anything a part of our mortal and spiritual experience can be put in the different Personality Profiles.

Question #5, under Reference section: A and B indicate Past time reference, C and D indicate Present time, and E and F indicate Future time. Meaning the time, you most focus on. More of the different letter questions indicate the following:

A) IDEALIST
Reference senses: A Sound and B Sight
Decision senses: D. Touch and F Smell

Motivator senses: E Taste and C Energy

B) CONCEPTUALIST
Reference senses: B Sight and A Sound
Decision senses: F Smell and D Touch
Motivator senses: C Energy and E Taste

C) ACTIONIST
Reference senses: C Energy and D Touch
Decision senses: B Sight and E Taste
Motivator senses: F Smell and A Sound

D) RELATIONALIST
Reference senses: D Touch and C Energy
Decision Senses: E Taste and B Sight
Motivator senses: A Sound and F Smell

E) FUNCTIONIST
Reference senses: E Taste and F Smell
Decision senses: A Sound and C Energy
Motivator senses: D Touch and B Sight

F) STRATEGIST
Reference Senses: F Smell and E Taste
Decision Senses: C Energy and A Sound
Motivator Senses: D Sight and B. Touch

IDEALIST

You are the thinkers for the world. Being driven to set direction for new pathways to increase life's meaning and add greater value. Life's focus for you is mostly on the past and you are constantly looking for more data and feedback the past may offer you.

You are a person who takes great action in your choices and always seeking more data for more wisdom in your choice.

Removing thoughts of the past from your mind is a natural pattern for you when you find greater value and meaning in something new.

Idealists believe that everyone has or must have their ideals and ethics. They are detail oriented to the point of being overly perfectionist. Often something is the best or worse, with no middle ground.

They believe in honor and live by a universal code of ethics. When they do not, it becomes a matter of pride - which they have too much of. They need to learn patience perfectly.

It is their ideal to manifest their ideals and objectives sooner than immediately. This sometimes gets in their way and so they have a tendency to jump ahead of themselves - trying to get to action (usually massive action) as quickly as possible.

Their philosophy is to live and act wisely in their striving to build and bring order to an imperfect world.

Idealists are the rarest type. They can be reclusive and oftentimes are very rich. Many live in England and Canada. A small percentage of Idealist live in the United States and other parts of the world.

IDEALIST FIRING ORDER:

1) Sound: Reference: Values and Meaning
2) Touch: Decision: Relationships
3) Taste: Motivator: Character, Processes
4) Sight: Reference: Ideas, Reason, Concepts
5) Smell: Decision: Strategies
6) Energy: Motivator: Action and Intuition

PHYSICS OF CLOSED SYSTEMS: ADDICTIONS

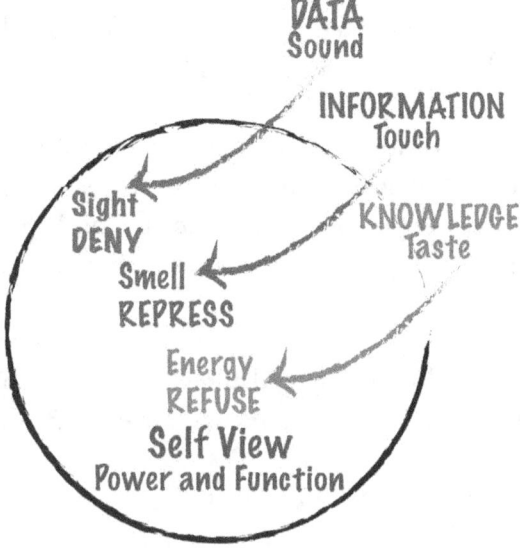

CONCEPTUALIST

You may be called a Visionary person, always able to see and gain ideas to aid others in life's directions. You are very logical and detailed in your thinking. Change can be easy for you especially when it pertains to the past.

There is very little that you miss about what goes on around you Though, you might struggle with the way it actually relates to you. You might struggle at times with intuitions you get especially when they mean you must question intuitions you've already had. The best way to deal with this is to question yourself about the current and past intuitions and take no action for a short time. It may be best to just wait and observe and the answer will appear.

Conceptualists are the "Brains" of the Human Family. They are the thinkers - extremely intelligent and very logical. They tend to be very disassociated and "digital" - having an insatiable appetite for information. They love books and reading.

Conceptualists have fond memories; especially regarding the glory of the past. They can also be quite self-righteous and stuck-up. They can easily become thick and stodgy, bureaucratic traditionalists.

Sometimes they are quirky and moody - having a low threshold for ambiguity, since they want to see the cause of things. They need to know that they know and feel powerless if they don't. This is very important to them because they are highly motivated to feel a great sense of personal power.

Many Conceptualists live in England and Canada. A small percentage of Conceptualist live in the United States and other parts of the world.

CONCEPTUALIST FIRING ORDER:

1) Sight: Reference: Ideas, Reason and Concepts
2) Smell: Decision: Strategies
3) Energy: Motivator: Actions and Intuitions
4) Sound: Reference: Values and Meaning
5) Touch: Decision: Relationships
6) Taste: Motivator: Character

Physics of Closed Systems: Addictions

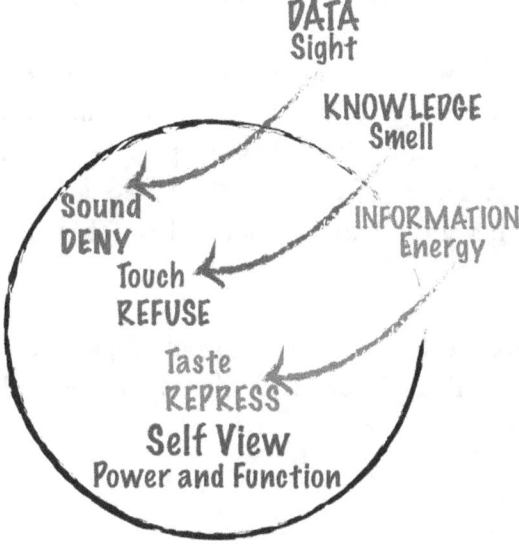

RELATIONALIST

You are focused in the present and you can be very loving and nurturing to the world around you. You are very informative about the way very different things in the world might relate to other things. You have a tendency to question yourself a lot and at times might find it difficult to recognize the role you play in the world around you.

Many people look for comfort though you're not confident always to see your own strengths in your ability to help them.

Because of this you are at times a bit codependent and this may be overcome by believing more in yourself and trusting your intuitions. You can also be strengthened by not taking actions always in the present but letting life fix itself.

Relationalists are people persons - they are natural net workers capable of building strong connections between themselves and others. They can be very nurturing and motherly as well as very achievement oriented.

Unfortunately, they want to maintain their relationships at all costs even at the cost of themselves. Many are co-dependent - enablers that are victims of their own self-sacrifice. This happens because they are usually Other Referenced. Their Life Challenge is to become their own authority. They feel that they are nothing without relationship. Some fall prey to self-deception.

Relationalist have a tendency to actively avoid people and things they don't like or relate to negatively. They will do this avoidance until some stimulus throws them into overwhelm.

There are three types of Relationalist:

A. The Helper: Someone that gives assistance, support. Such as an extra locomotive attached to a train at the front, middle or rear. The Helper is someone that stimulates another directly as a signal. The Helper gives or renders aid, assistance or service directly or indirectly.

B. The Counter-Exemplar: The Counter-Exemplar go contrary to the standard model sometimes in a reverse, opposite or contrary direction in opposition. These people might respond opposing and refuting at times. When mature they are very original archetypes such as Plato and other great path builders.

C. The Achiever: Also called The Chief. Achievers are naturally successful to an end result being able to see things through to completion. They attain by great effort they put forth and usually come out victorious. Especially when they have a purpose, they bring about the intended conclusion.

Relationalist make up over 55% of the American Population, as well as the vast majority of Hispanics and Europeans like the French, the Germans, and Italians. Most all blacks are also Relationalist.

RELATIONSALIST FIRING ORDER:

1) Touch: Reference: Touch
2) Taste: Decision: Character
3) Sound: Motivator: Values and Meaning
4) Energy: Reference: Action and Intuition
5) Sight: Decision: Ideas, Reasons, Concepts
6) Smell: Motivator: Strategies

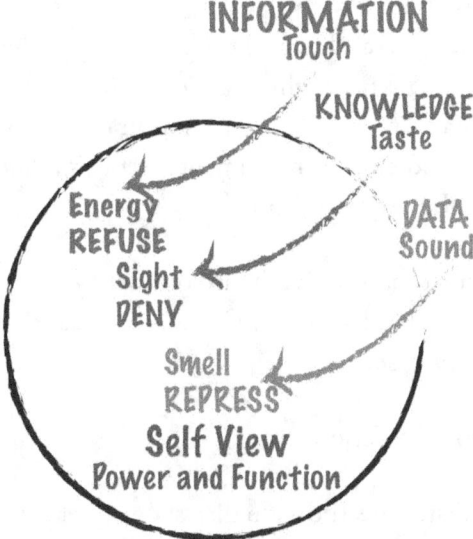

ACTIONIST

You are very intuitive though take action too quickly and with too much emotion. Take some time to just see what may happen before taking action then do take action. You have a problem with allowing others to assist you and you don't rely enough on relationships you already have. You can even be stubborn at times.

You are a library of information and motivated for more knowledge for the future. You offer your knowing freely to the world with the reasons and steps for applying the knowledge.

Actionists are individualists that enjoy their unique special ness - they like being different. For them their word is their bond. They often sacrifice themselves to keep a promise. They are the world's biggest doubters and can seem miserly, selfish, and overly self-centered ice men or maidens. They frequently suffer from being envious.

Unlike Relationalist they have a hard time maintaining the connection with others. They often feel they live the tragic life of the misunderstood romantic. If they don't know which action to take, they are unwilling and many times unable to act. Being in motion means living - it signifies purpose. Many are addicted to movement (Actions). They have an issue with anger and can be very wrathful.

They are motivated to be the living embodiment of their ideals and are constantly refining and redefining their knowledge and skills. Actionists, if mature can be very wise.

There are three types of Actionists:

A. The Individualist: The Individualist shows great independence and individuality in thought and actions. They advocate for individuality and individualism and are sensitive to particular characteristics distinguishing self from others. These for them are a principle and habit to a point, at times of not pursuing common or collective interests.

B. The Observer: The Observer is good at just observing and being able to report happenings and events. They merely observe, this can cause others to not always appreciate them as they seldom get involved personally. They have a natural tendency to report events and happenings as they might observe them approaching the situation. The Observer does pay close attention to many things and usually considers carefully many events happening at one time.

C. The Doer: The Doer is always doing something and will get things done with vigor and efficiency. They are characterized by action and distinguished from one given to contemplation. The Doer generally has an amusing or eccentric character.

Most of the people of Scandinavia and Holland are Actionists. They represent roughly 25% of the American Population, many of them Hispanics.

ACTIONIST FIRING ORDER:

1) Energy: Reference: Actions and Intuition
2) Sight: Decision: Ideas, Reason and Concepts
3) Smell: Motivator: Strategies
4) Touch: Reference: Relationships
5) Taste: Decision: Character
6) Sound: Motivator: Values and Meaning

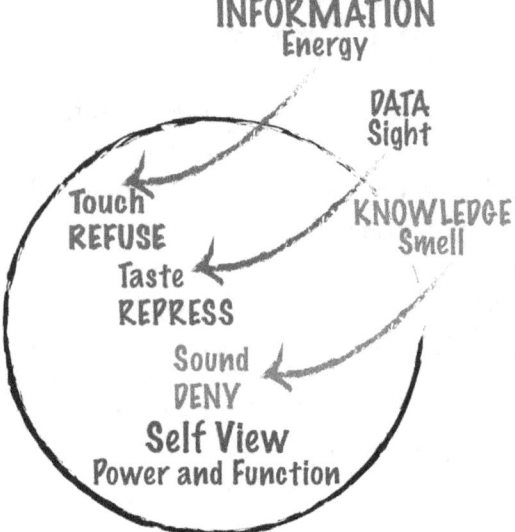

FUNCTIONIST

Functionist make up 75% of the world population. You are good at business and your main focus is always for tomorrow's success plans. You can seem a bit cold in your personal relationships at times. Your view of the world is based upon processes values and relationship so you can be very dedicated to family and friends. Your view of yourself is the step by step instructions for accomplishment so you can be somewhat self-critical. You might also question your own actions and intuitions and have trouble with your reasons for doing these.

Functionist put things together. They work on problems by using their great capacity to absorb and digest enormous amounts of data. Their random, yet systematic processing forms organized structures whose parts work together like finely meshed gears.

They are motivated to seek out the most important ideas and feel stymied when they take these solutions and find that they can't work it out into a plan. Their first thought is safety and security, so they find ways of circumventing discomfort and pain. They are consistently finding ways to make life better, but unfortunately, they can fall into greed and gluttony as they strive to feel good.

These powerful people have an insatiable curiosity and so usually develop a diverse range of interests and tastes. Although they sometimes tend to be optimistic dreamers and a bit naive, this is tempered by their practical side.

Functionist, in groups, tend to strive for uniformity yet can be respectful of personal idiosyncrasies.

Most of the Japanese are Functionist. Some North and South American Indian tribes are made up of mostly Functionist. It has been discovered that some Irish people of Celtic Origins are of the type also.

FUNCTIONIST FIRING ORDER:

1) Taste: Reference: Character
2) Sound: Decision: Values and Meaning
3) Touch; Motivator: Relationships
4) Smell: Reference: Strategies
5) Energy: Decision: Actions and Intuition
6) Sight: Motivator: Ideas, Reason and Concept

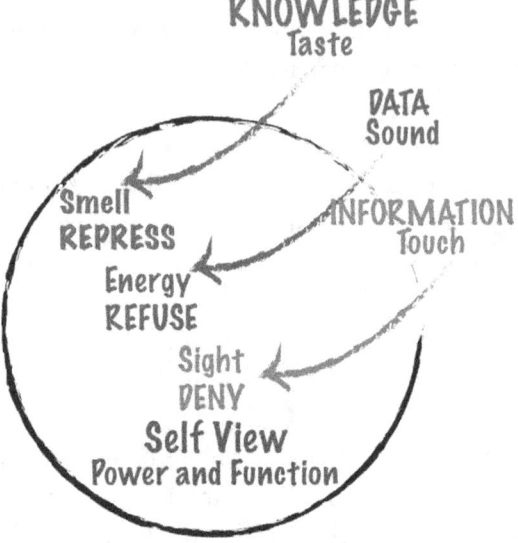

STRATEGIST

You are very rare and have great capability of being rich in whatever course you choose in life. You have great knowledge and know when to act or when to question before you action. You are seen by others for your great abilities though you don't always recognize these in yourself.

Strategists are planners - tacticians that work things out sequentially. They prize competency and are guardians of skill - being dedicated and hardworking individuals that thrive on tight schedules.

They have basic life issues with money and risking - and sometimes sex. Because they like the "sweet smell of Success", they live with the ever-present danger of falling into lust and avarice.

Strategists are afraid of doing things wrong and not fitting in. They sometimes have a hard time finding what feels good to them. To compensate for their lack of self-confidence with others, they continually look for ways of connecting with a group that has stable, well-defined values.

They are very loyal to others they respect and admire. There is a heart of Gold at the end of their rainbow.

Most of the Chinese, the Taiwanese, and the Tibetans are of the type - making them the highest percentage of the world's population. Some North and South American Indian Tribes are made up mostly of Strategists.

You might struggle at times with your relationship with God.

STRATEGIST FIRING ORDER:

1) Smell: Reference: Strategies
2) Energy: Decision: Actions and Intuition
3) Sight: Motivator: Ideas, Reason and Concept
4) Taste: Reference: Character
5) Sound: Decision: Values and Meaning
6) Touch: Motivator: Relationships

Strategist Closed System

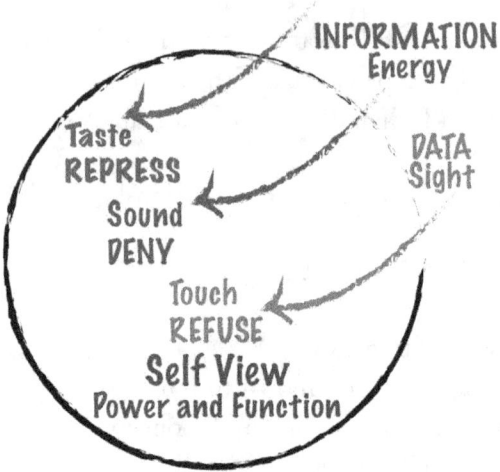

CHAPTER 4

PHYSICS OF ADDICTIONS

Open and Closed Systems is a Physics Theory and consists of Physics Laws. It has many applications and the simple fact remains that a Closed System, of any kind, is an Addicted System.

Closed Systems are not open to new feedback, data or information, let alone knowledge; their boundaries are neither flexible nor permeable. Closed systems do not grow nor gain anything; they head toward self-destruction and eventually implode if they do not open up. This happens in the human body between our cells, when cells boundaries close off and are not permeable it becomes cancerous and infects other cells. Cells must communicate with one another, when a cell cannot send a signal out or cannot receive a signal, disease is the result. This ability to send and receive communication is through the membrane or boundary of the cells. A closed boundary (closed system) self-destructs the cell and the systems inter-related and inter-dependent on the cell for communication. When a Closed System is in decline, Natural forces come into play and their only goal is to eliminate or lift the restrictions that keep the System Closed. These natural forces can feel like battering rams pounding on the boundaries and walls of the Closed System. This, at times, can appear as natural consequences of choice, forcing the Whole System towards "hitting rock bottom". Hitting rock bottom is the Natural forces last resort at eliminating or lifting the restrictions that are keeping the System Closed.

I have experienced "tough love" and I have "hit rock bottom" in my past, and I survived. I have worked with many addicts and have had to impose and encourage others to take a stand in the name of love. I have seen many great individuals hit "rock bottom", I have even been to a few funerals of beautiful, talented, bright, loving addicts. Are you through being a Survivor and ready to live yet?

Stability becomes dysfunctional because a Closed System can only duplicate itself, therefore Closed Systems become generational, Addictive Systems, and communities.

All systems are intended to be Open Systems. There are two main functions of the human senses in regard to the physics of a system. There is specific sensory data acting as a natural force to change other sensory data's effect on the individual. The only true function of our sensory data regarding our system as a whole being is to create a specific "view". The "view" itself is not the reality of our self nor the world around us; this view created through our sensory experience is just our range of vision or examination of our self and the world we live in. Your range of vision will not go beyond your pre-programmed beliefs and views, what you view is what you have within. To be able to actually experience the self and the world is virtually impossible for a closed system. An actual experience of the world and the self is a direct observation of and participation in events as a basis of knowledge.

Experiencing is a state of being affected by and gaining knowledge through the observation and participation of the events around us. Not denying, refusing, repressing and avoiding them. Experience is something we personally encounter, undergo and live through and gain greater knowledge and growth from.

There are other physics principles necessary to "experience" instead of just "view" and these consist of: Entropy Cycle, Totalities and Quantum Bridging. You must first Be an Open System to even allow these other principles to work in your life. If you are not open none of this will help to change you. Justifying or denying, refusing to learn is a closed system and is addicted to their own thought patterns and emotions and behavioral patterns. If you are predictable in the responses to make to things, you are closed. The hope is that just knowing this information alone can help to make you more open and may motivate you to believe and dream again. No one closes off intentionally we are born open, our life's experiences cause us to close off. The actual application of these physics principles along with the knowledge enables you to transform.

Otherwise, to just "view" our world and to just "view" the self is simply an opinion or judgments based upon feelings and thoughts from our past experiences and the subconscious programs regarding those. Change is practically impossible; we feel lucky to have a step by step change (incremental change). Holographic Human Transformation Theory is based upon the 4 physics principles mentioned and is functional based upon the physics of correspondence. These 4 physics principles are mentioned in this book, and there are separate books going into great detail about the physics laws and Holographic Human Transformation Theory.

This might sound like a lot especially at first, but when broken down and over lain on the Holographic Human Theory its affect is Identity level change. The ability to actually "experience" the world and to "experience" our self rather than just "view" them is a whole higher level of consciousness. To be an observer and to participate in the events around us and to do so in such a manner that the self continually gains greater knowledge.

Physic laws of Open vs. Closed System as applied to Holographic Human Transformation Theory:

The first three senses fired in the Holographic Human Theory firing order are the individuals World View. This is based upon your sensory firing order in your Personality Profile you did in Chapter 3. The first 3 sense along with the sensory primary functions, the major and minor meta programs and the different elements of the different totalities. All of these aspects from the different senses have an exact effect on our natural being from a subconscious level. The world view from the first 3 senses fired is our personal view of the world around us, in other words, our personal world view. It contains, beliefs, opinions, thoughts, emotions and behaviors that we perceive judge and decided about simply based upon the sensory functions and programs.

The self-view is the last 3 senses fired in the firing order and the world view is the view that is programmed to view in order to get the self-view to overcome its weaknesses and to gain greater knowledge. This is the whole purpose of an open system: to continue to grow and gain more knowledge from our life experience. Whatever weakness the self-view consists of is automatically what the worldview will see to trigger the self-view for an opportunity to change. As the self-view does grow and gain knowledge more and more experiences are available to be seen from a greater knowledge view in the worldview. The closed system continues to see things that trigger the self-view, but the worldview denies its validity, it refuses to accept the world view event as something it needs or lacks and finds ways to repress it at any cost. This in turn leaves the self-view living and viewing its weaknesses and not growing nor gaining greater knowledge.

This World View, based upon the human senses firing to have the view, are just natural forces coming into play to remove our self-view's limiting beliefs. What?!? What is viewed in the world by the individual is what is needed to remove limiting beliefs of the self?!?! What we see, and judge of the world serves the purpose of lifting the "view" of our self so we may experience "Self", as the self truly is. The more severely we judge the world the greater the natural forces of that view become because the limitations of the self-view are so restrictive. We are so much more inside ourselves than can imagine let alone realize (real eyes) that we are.

It is the world view that triggers the dysfunctional patterns and programs of the self-view that are in direct correlation with the limitations of the self-view. Our own self view limitations are our own dysfunctional patterns and programs that keep us from experiencing our true self. If you feel or notice your life's patterns just repeating themselves somehow, it is a result of being a closed system and not growing and gaining greater knowledge through life's events and experiences.

When we can change the world view, we then automatically change the self-view dysfunctional programs and remove those self-view limitations. When this begins to occur, we begin to experience our world as our self and begin to become more knowledgeable and wiser through life's events.

These physics laws are easily understood using examples in our life when we have viewed our world around us as hostile or unfair in some way to us. Our internal (self-view) program might become defensive or withdrawn. Either program doesn't address the world view. When we view the world around us (even if they are picking on us) as an opportunity to grow and to overcome our dysfunctional patterns, we may respond by learning to express our self, more detailed. There are many examples of the way you have viewed the world and its effect on your self-view or internal program response. Whatever the view might be; fear, anger, not understood, Face the View. Admit, accept, and express to grow and to overcome the self-view limitations.

The Self-View limiting patterns are to help an individual avoid the unavoidable, The True Self. Why might one choose to avoid their true self? We all have limiting beliefs we acquired through our upbringing and our life experiences. We all have weaknesses; it is our own self-limiting beliefs keeping us from becoming all we may become. It is only the self we must learn to overcome. We are our greatest enemy. Natural man is an enemy of God and of the self. Our weaknesses are to become our strengths. Avoid the weaknesses within instead of face them and turn them into strengths. Deny them. Refuse to accept them. Repress them. We are already convinced they do not exist. If life's patterns (events, experiences, views) repeat themselves, we are denying, refusing and repressing our true self and our world view is working to get us to face ourselves. You will not stand before God one day and blame others for your responses and weaknesses.

The True Self appears to have missing parts based upon the self-view. Remove the limits in self-view and remember the True Self. The missing parts were never missing at all, they were just restricted from your view. Removing these limitations allows you to experience and not just view the self. The self-view's true-self is within, the limitations are restraints holding the true-self back. Something has set a limit, a boundary, stipulations as to not allowing you to be your true-self, this true-self knows itself and seeks to remove these boundaries. The true-self needs assistance and the worldview is attempting to assist.

A Closed Systems is a Totality and consists of three separate Elements the three Elements of a Closed System are: Deny, Refuse and Repress. Deny is associated with the senses of sound and sight; literally what we hear and see. Deny is also then associated with the functions, meta-programs and elements associated with the sense of sound and sight: values, ethics, meaning, ideas, reasons, mental processes and concepts. Refuse is associated with the sense of touch and energy, their functions, meta-programs and elements: relationships, intuitions, actions and emotions. Repress is associated with the sense of taste and smell, their functions, meta-programs and elements: beliefs about character, processes, belief about strategies, and behaviors.

An Open System is a Totality and consists of three separate Elements the three Elements of an Open System are Admit, Accept and Express. Admit is associated with the sense of sound and sight; literally all we hear and see. Admit is then associated with the functions, meta-programs, and elements associated with these senses: values, ethics, meanings, ideas, reasons, concepts and mental processes. Accept is associated with the sense of touch and energy, their functions, meta-programs and elements: relationships, intuitions, actions and emotions. Express is associated with the sense of taste and smell and their functions, meta-programs and elements: beliefs about character, processes, beliefs about strategies and behaviors.

Each Element of any Totality has specific human senses they are associated with and functioning in relation to. Each Element of any Totality has its own identity and function which is very important to the totality they make. If the elements are not functioning properly together, the Totality is also not functional.

Physics of Closed Systems: Addictions

All Systems and Elements work together based upon the Physics of Correspondence. The simple version of Correspondence is the open ability of each of the senses and the elements associated with the senses to correspond together. Correspondence breaks down to a mathematical correlation between different sets with different functions. Correspondence is a relationship between sets in which each member of the one set is associated with one or more member of the other set. In other words, the different senses with their different functions, meta-program and elements must correspond with one another for the whole system (whole human being) to function properly to its potential. This corresponding must be inter-relating and inter-dependent so as to maintain the individual identity of each of the senses, their functions, meta-programs and elements. Just as in the Totality (3 Elements) of Time. Past (Element 1) is associated with the sense of sound and sight. Present (Element 2) is associated with the sense of touch and energy. Future (Element 3) is associated with the sense of taste and smell. Past is the Past, do not bring it into the Present or Future. Present is the Present, do not put it in the Past or Future. Future is the Future, do not put it in the Past or Present. Still, they do inter-relate, inter-dependently in order for the Totality potential of Time itself to be a whole system in our lives. Some people actually struggle with whether they have a future or whether their past can ever be overcome and might feel as though they are not living in their present.

Each Element of an open or closed system affects the specific functions and associated Elements within that human sense. There are over 30 Totalities with 3 Elements per each Totality that are identified, and each element is associated with 2 human senses as shown with the Closed vs. Open Systems and Time Totalities.

Stability is dysfunctional and indicates a Closed System. Stability as in firmness or a resistance to change is dysfunctional in an Open System. Stability indicating changelessness, uniformity and invariability indicates a closed system. Everything in life that is progressive becomes stagnant when it holds firmly to its original state or condition.

The Far From Equilibrium State (FELS) is part of the natural forces coming into play to remove the self-view limitations. The Far From Equilibrium State is the "hitting rock bottom" that is spoken of regarding any addiction, this is whereby all outwards appearances you can no longer: Deny, Refuse nor Repress the feedback from the environment. On a quantum physics-Holographic Human Transformation basis it is explained as the closed system imploding. This is an inward burst of the whole system, considered a violent compression to collapse inward as if from the outward pressures. This is a break-down of falling apart from within: All the denial and factors of the closed system become the center: the world view with all its denial and closed system functions becomes the self-view and the self-view becomes the world view. The imploded closed systems see's all the pain and suffering it has inflicted upon others through all its denial, refusal, and repressing. The world view as the self-view, now feels worthless, hopeless, and unforgivable. All the weaknesses in the world view were trying to turn into strengths and are the new self-views world view of themselves in the world. This FELS is a Totality and consists of three separate Elements: Stability, Chaos, Randomness (complete disorder). The 3 elements of this natural force are sensory associated as are all the elements. Stability is associated with the sense of sound and sight and their functions, meta-programs and elements: stability in all we hear and see and, in our values, meaning, ideas, reasons, thoughts and our Past. Set firmly about these things and their original state or condition. The FELS Totality and its Elements will indicate the degree of limitations of Self View.

Self-View naturally sympathizes and indulges practices and beliefs (for self) which are different or in conflict with the True Self.

The FELS purpose is to take the World View to the Randomness or complete disorder state at this state the Closed System bursts. Self-View becomes World View and we finally perceive the Self as the World view has been attempting to get us to view. This is a function of Detox on the human system for someone addicted to substances. This is the physics behind their change in personal behavior, so much of their dysfunctional patterns just seeming to go away after they complete the detox process.

The World View becomes quite different and their Self View limitations are temporarily removed.

There are numerous examples of the application of the physics principle between a person's world view and their dysfunctional programs. A closed system doesn't just willingly admit that their dysfunctional reactions to things are their own programs. It is blamed upon something or someone in their environment; they may take some blame but justifiably and repress their own fault.

Creating the Far from Equilibrium State for a Closed System accelerates the removal of the Self-View limitations. This means that the World View must give the Closed System Data and Feedback to take the Self-View to a state of complete Disorder. In this state of complete disorder, the True Self can no longer be denied.

Holographic Human Transformation Theory identifies the senses, their functions and each Element and its function to easily walk you through the areas to focus on the Elements apply. This state of complete disorder is associated with the sense of taste and smell and their functions, meta-programs and elements; Beliefs about character, processes, strategies, behaviors and their future. Not all addicts are easily taken to this Far From Equilibrium State. Still, there are many different approaches for helping to accomplish this through the different Totalities and their Elements. There are many choices for approach for different closed systems, still to search for an approach of creating this for them rather than just letting the natural forces bring it about may be much safer for everyone involved.

The Far From Equilibrium State placed on the Holographic Human Transformation Theory correlates in the following patterns for a Closed System:

1st Element: Stability: Sound and Sight, values, meaning, ideas, reasons, Mental Processes, Denying, (opposite of deny is admit), Past.

2nd Element: Chaos: Touch and Energy: relationships, intuitions, emotional processes, Refuse (opposite of refuse, is accept), Present.

3rd Element: Randomness: complete disorder, taste and smell, beliefs about character and processes, beliefs about strategies, behavioral processes, Repress (opposite of repress is express), Future.

These 3 Elements of the FELS (Far from Equilibrium State) can be applied to create the state of complete disorder ("hitting rock bottom"). If you choose to use this approach always make sure you have options of help when they hit rock bottom. Becoming an Open System, yourself is essential in helping another. A closed system can only duplicate itself and the addict is already a closed system they must be worked with by an open system to become open themselves and move beyond their addiction.

A Closed System is an Addicted System and can only duplicate other Addicted Systems (Closed Systems).

Closed Systems boundaries are not flexible or permeable anything the world is trying to tell them is simply denied by the closed system or the closed system just refuses to even acknowledge the feedback at all and eventually absolutely represses the feedback and won't even put up with the worlds attempts of feedback to it. Comments like: "Never contact me again", "I am sick of you just leave me alone." They can even just disappear for long periods of time with zero to little contact with people that care.

If you are a Closed System and you are attempting to help a Closed System that has become addicted to substances, you cannot help. A Closed System can only duplicate itself. You must first become an Open System yourself before you can help someone with an addiction.

Reading and studying this book, doing the assignments and exercises repetitively and applying all you learn may help you become an Open System.

EXERCISE/ASSIGNMENT FOR CHAPTER 4

Congratulations, you have already faced one of the hardest, the monster under the bed, so to speak yourself. Keep going and you will find that monster's strength and ancient wisdom.

Find a place and time you can be by yourself for at least 30 minutes during the day. Have a pen and make a list at least 7 each of the following: desires, goals, dreams and needs as you can remember. Go back, in your memories to as young as you can remember or imagine, and up to the time you think you might have become the "Closed System" to the degree you scored on the Closed System Evaluation in Chapter 2.

Make a list of seven desires, goals, dreams and needs which may have seemed or seem "fairy-tale" like or impossible, even at the time. Let your imagination soar, let go of your fears and boundaries for just a time and imagine to dream your greatest dreams. The Lord once said, "anything they can imagine, they can do." So, imagine or pretend to imagine your deepest dreams, desires, and goals.

List any and every desire, goal, and dream and need you may remember, small and large. Think just in the terms of imagining for now, achievable or seemingly impossible. List these for yourself, even as they might pertain to your achieving them for others. Be sure to guess or estimate the time which you had these and list this also. Time is an important Element in our lives and time is as much a part of change as choice is.

List all you can remember or imagine right up to the time and/or event which you think might have been the "last straw" that put you into your current "Closed" state of being.

Begin this in the morning and spend time during the day pondering it. Whenever you think of more, write them down. Do this exercise, remembering and writing them down.

Ask at least 3 other people who knew you back then what of your desires, goals, dreams, and needs they may remember of you or may have imagined themselves of you.

You must list at least 7 of each to complete this assignment. Include by the item you list the approximate age you were when you had this item you listed.

ENJOY THE JOURNEY

EVALUATIONS FOR HOLOGRAPHIC HUMAN MODELS

SENSORY PERSONALITY PREFERENCE

The following lists are different aspects of the "Self" categorized into the different Personality Profiles. From your Personality Profile determination, you can see on the following list the different parts of yourself in the different sensory programs in your Sensory firing order.

This may take some repetition of studying and then may be very useful regarding the various aspects and their sensory areas where you may gain ideas of helping yourself overcome.

(Reference points are always of the same Elements and other Major Meta. Reference, Decision and Motivator points are 1 of each of the other 4 senses).

CONCEPTULIST

Sight: Reference

Based upon what is seen through this sense. Primary Question; Why; (Reasons, Ideas, Concepts) Major Meta: Delete (difference).

Elements: Mental: (Human Consciousness), Past: (Time), Data:(Wisdom), Take Action: (Choice), Direction:(Change), Individual: (Worldview), Real: (Memory), Identity: (Human Function), Structure: (Nature), Wrong: (Quantum), Intent: (Message), Reception: (Data processing sequence), Deny: (Closed System), Admit: (Open System), Delete: (Transformation).

Smell: Decision

Based upon what is smelled through this sense. Primary Question; Where. (Strategies) Major Meta: Generalize (sameness).

Elements: Physical: (Human Consciousness), Future: (Time), Knowledge: (Wisdom), Let others take action: (Choice), Modeling: (Change), Society: (Worldview), Genetic: (Memory), Creation: (Human Function), Processes: (Nature), Death: (Quantum), Context: (Message), Transmit: (Data processing sequence), Repress: (Closed System), Express: (Open System), Permutation: (Transformation).

Energy: Motivator

Based upon what actions in the environment and within you, also intuitions you have. Primary Question; Which. (Action, Intuition) Major Meta: Distort (diminish),

Elements: Emotions: (Human Consciousness), Present: (Time), Information: (Wisdom), No Action: (Choice), Question: (Change), Family: (Worldview), Vicarious: (Memory), Communication: (Human Function), Patterns: (Nature), Self: (Quantum), Content: (Message), Storage: (Data processing sequence), Refuse: (Closed System), Accept: (Open System), Insert: (Transformation).

Sound: Reference:

Based upon anything heard through this sense whether environmental or internal, such as thoughts: Primary Question; What; (Values, Ethics, Meaning) Major Meta: Delete (sameness).

Elements: Mental: (Human Consciousness), Past: (Time), Data: (Wisdom), Take Action: (Choice), Direction: (Change), Individual: (Worldview), Real: (Memory), Identity: (Human Function), Structure: (Nature), Right: (Quantum), Intent: (Message), Reception: (Data processing sequence), Deny: (Closed System), Admit: (Open System), Delete: (Transformation).

Touch: Decision

Based upon anything felt through this sense: Primary Question; Who; (Relationships, the way things relate with each other), Major Meta: Distort (Amplification).

Elements: Emotions: (Human Consciousness), Present:(Time), Information: (Wisdom), No Action: (Choice), Question: (Change), Family: (Worldview), Vicarious: (Memory), Communication: (Human Function), Patterns: (Nature), God: (Quantum), Content: (Message), Storage: (Data processing sequence), Refuse: (Closed System), Accept: (Open System), Insert: (Transformation).

Taste: Motivator

Based upon anything experienced by this sense: Primary Question; How; (Belief about character, identifying character), Major Meta: Generalize (difference).

Elements: Physical: (Human Consciousness), Future: (Time), Knowledge: (Wisdom), Let others take action: (Choice), Modeling: (Change), Society: (Worldview), Genetic: (Memory), Creation: (Human Function), Processes: (Nature), Life: (Quantum), Context: (Message), Transmit: (Data processing sequence), Repress: (Closed System), Express: (Open System), Permutation: (Transformation).

IDEALIST

Sound: Reference

Based upon anything heard through this sense whether environmental or internal, such as thoughts: Primary Question is What. (Values, Ethics, Meaning) Major Meta: Delete (sameness).

Elements: Mental: (Human Consciousness), Past: (Time), Data: (Wisdom), Take Action: (Choice), Direction: (Change), Individual: (Worldview), Real: (Memory), Identity: (Human Function), Structure: (Nature), Right: (Quantum), Intent: (Message), Reception: (Data processing sequence), Deny: (Closed System), Admit: (Open System), Delete: (Transformation).

Touch: Decision

Based upon anything felt through this sense: Primary Question is Who (Relationships, the way things relate with each other), Major Meta: Distort (Amplification).

Elements: Emotions: (Human Consciousness), Present: (Time), Information: (Wisdom), No Action: (Choice), Question: (Change), Family: (Worldview), Vicarious: (Memory), Communication: (Human Function), Patterns: (Nature), God: (Quantum), Content: (Message), Storage: (Data processing sequence), Refuse: (Closed System), Accept: (Open System), Insert: (Transformation).

Taste: Motivator

Based upon anything experienced by this sense: Primary Question is How. (Belief about character, identifying character), Major Meta: Generalize (difference).

Elements: Physical: (Human Consciousness), Future: (Time), Knowledge: (Wisdom), Let others take action: (Choice), Modeling: (Change), Society: (Worldview), Genetic: (Memory), Creation: (Human Function), Processes: (Nature), Life: (Quantum), Context: (Message), Transmit: (Data processing sequence), Repress: (Closed System), Express: (Open System), Permutation: (Transformation).

Sight: Reference

Based upon what is seen through this sense. Primary Question is Why, (Reasons, Ideas, Concepts) Major Meta: Delete (difference).

Elements: Mental: (Human Consciousness), Past: (Time), Data: (Wisdom), Take Action: (Choice), Direction: (Change), Individual: (Worldview), Real: (Memory), Identity: (Human Function), Structure: (Nature), Wrong: (Quantum), Intent: (Message), Reception: (Data processing sequence), Deny: (Closed System), Admit: (Open System), Delete: (Transformation).

Smell: Decision

Based upon what is smelled through this sense. Primary Question is Where. (Strategies) Major Meta: Generalize (sameness).

Elements: Physical: (Human Consciousness), Future: (Time), Knowledge: (Wisdom), Let others take action: (Choice), Modeling: (Change), Society: (Worldview), Genetic: (Memory), Creation: (Human Function), Processes: (Nature), Death: (Quantum), Context: (Message), Transmit: (Data processing sequence), Repress: (Closed System), Express: (Open System), Permutation: (Transformation)

Energy: Motivator

Based upon what actions in the environment and within you, also intuitions you have. Primary Question is Which. (Action, Intuition) Major Meta: Distort (diminish).

Elements: Emotions: (Human Consciousness), Present: (Time), Information: (Wisdom), No Action: (Choice), Question: (Change), Family: (Worldview), Vicarious: (Memory), Communication: (Human Function), Patterns: (Nature), Self: (Quantum), Content: (Message), Storage: (Data processing sequence), Refuse: (Closed System), Accept: (Open System), Insert: (Transformation).

RELATIONALIST

Touch: Reference

Based upon anything felt through this sense: Primary Question is Who (Relationships, the way things relate with each other), Major Meta: Distort (Amplification).

Elements: Emotions: (Human Consciousness), Present: (Time), Information: (Wisdom), No Action: (Choice), Question: (Change), Family: (Worldview), Vicarious: (Memory), Communication: (Human Function), Patterns: (Nature), God: (Quantum), Content: (Message), Storage: (Data processing sequence), Refuse: (Closed System), Accept: (Open System), Insert: (Transformation).

Taste: Decision

Based upon anything experienced by this sense: Primary Question is How. (Belief about character, identifying character), Major Meta: Generalize (difference).

Elements: Physical: (Human Consciousness), Future: (Time), Knowledge: (Wisdom), Let others take action: (Choice), Modeling: (Change), Society: (Worldview), Genetic: (Memory), Creation: (Human Function), Processes: (Nature), Life: (Quantum), Context: (Message), Transmit: (Data processing sequence), Repress: (Closed System), Express: (Open System), Permutation: (Transformation)

Sound: Motivator

Based upon anything heard through this sense whether environmental or internal, such as thoughts: Primary Question is What. (Values, Ethics, Meaning) Major Meta: Delete (sameness).

Elements: Mental: (Human Consciousness), Past: (Time), Data: (Wisdom), Take Action: (Choice), Direction: (Change), Individual: (Worldview), Real: (Memory), Identity: (Human Function), Structure: (Nature), Right: (Quantum), Intent: (Message), Reception: (Data processing sequence), Deny: (Closed System), Admit: (Open System), Delete: (Transformation).

Energy: Reference

Based upon what actions in the environment and within you, also intuitions you have. Primary Question is Which. (Action, Intuition) Major Meta: Distort (Diminish).

Elements: Emotions: (Human Consciousness), Present: (Time), Information: (Wisdom), No Action: (Choice), Question: (Change), Family: (Worldview), Vicarious: (Memory), Communication: (Human Function), Patterns: (Nature), Self: (Quantum), Content: (Message), Storage: (Data processing sequence), Refuse: (Closed System), Accept: (Open System), Insert: (Transformation).

Sight: Reference

Based upon what is seen through this sense. Primary Question is Why, (Reasons, Ideas, Concepts) Major Meta: Delete (difference).

Elements: Mental: (Human Consciousness), Past: (Time), Data: (Wisdom), Take Action: (Choice), Direction: (Change), Individual: (Worldview), Real: (Memory), Identity: (Human Function), Structure: (Nature), Wrong: (Quantum), Intent: (Message), Reception: (Data processing sequence), Deny: (Closed System), Admit: (Open System), Delete: (Transformation).

Smell: Motivator

Based upon what is smelled through this sense. Primary Question is Where. (Strategies) Major Meta: Generalize (sameness).

Elements: Physical: (Human Consciousness), Future: (Time), Knowledge: (Wisdom), Let others take action: (Choice), Modeling: (Change), Society:

(Worldview), Genetic: (Memory), Creation: (Human Function), Processes: (Nature), Death: (Quantum), Context: (Message), Transmit: (Data processing sequence), Repress: (Closed System), Express: (Open System), Permutation: (Transformation).

ACTIONIST

Energy: Reference

Based upon what actions in the environment and within you, also intuitions you have. Primary Question is Which. (Action, Intuition) Major Meta: Distort (diminish).

Elements: Emotions: (Human Consciousness), Present: (Time), Information: (Wisdom), No Action: (Choice), Question: (Change), Family: (Worldview), Vicarious: (Memory), Communication: (Human Function), Patterns: (Nature), Self: (Quantum), Content: (Message), Storage: (Data processing sequence), Refuse: (Closed System), Accept: (Open System), Insert: (Transformation).

Sight: Decision

Based upon what is seen through this sense. Primary Question is Why, (Reasons, Ideas, Concepts) Major Meta: Delete (difference).

Elements: Mental: (Human Consciousness), Past: (Time), Data: (Wisdom), Take Action: (Choice), Direction: (Change), Individual: (Worldview), Real: (Memory), Identity: (Human Function), Structure: (Nature), Wrong: (Quantum), Intent: (Message), Reception: (Data processing sequence), Deny: (Closed System), Admit: (Open System), Delete: (Transformation).

Smell: Motivator

Based upon what is smelled through this sense. Primary Question is Where. (Strategies) Major Meta: Generalize (sameness).

Elements: Physical: (Human Consciousness), Future: (Time), Knowledge: (Wisdom), Let others take action: (Choice), Modeling: (Change), Society: (Worldview), Genetic: (Memory), Creation: (Human Function), Processes: (Nature), Death: (Quantum), Context: (Message), Transmit: (Data processing sequence), Repress: (Closed System), Express: (Open System), Permutation: (Transformation).

Touch: Reference

Based upon anything felt through this sense: Primary Question is Who (Relationships, the way things relate with each other), Major Meta: Distort (Amplification).

Elements: Emotions: (Human Consciousness), Present: (Time), Information: (Wisdom), No Action: (Choice), Question: (Change), Family: (Worldview), Vicarious: (Memory), Communication: (Human Function), Patterns: (Nature), God: (Quantum), Content: (Message), Storage: (Data processing sequence), Refuse: (Closed System), Accept: (Open System), Insert: (Transformation).

Taste: Decision

Based upon anything experienced by this sense: Primary Question is How. (Belief about character, identifying character), Major Meta: Generalize (difference).

Elements: Physical: (Human Consciousness), Future: (Time), Knowledge: (Wisdom), Let others take action: (Choice), Modeling: (Change), Society: (Worldview), Genetic: (Memory), Creation: (Human Function), Processes: (Nature), Life: (Quantum), Context: (Message), Transmit: (Data processing sequence), Repress: (Closed System), Express: (Open System), Permutation: (Transformation).

Sound: Motivator

Based upon anything heard through this sense whether environmental or internal, such as thoughts: Primary Question is What. (Values, Ethics, Meaning) Major Meta: Delete (sameness).

Elements: Mental: (Human Consciousness), Past: (Time), Data: (Wisdom), Take Action: (Choice), Direction: (Change), Individual: (Worldview), Real: (Memory), Identity: (Human Function), Structure: (Nature), Right: (Quantum), Intent: (Message), Reception: (Data processing sequence), Deny: (Closed System), Admit: (Open System), Delete: (Transformation).

STRATEGIST

Smell: Reference

Based upon what is smelled through this sense. Primary Question is Where. (Strategies) Major Meta: Generalize (sameness).

Elements: Physical: (Human Consciousness), Future: (Time), Knowledge: (Wisdom), Let others take action: (Choice), Modeling: (Change), Society: (Worldview), Genetic: (Memory), Creation: (Human Function), Processes: (Nature), Death: (Quantum), Context: (Message), Transmit: (Data processing sequence), Repress: (Closed System), Express: (Open System), Permutation: (Transformation)

Energy: Decision

Based upon what actions in the environment and within you, also intuitions you have. Primary Question is Which. (Action, Intuition) Major Meta: Distort (diminish).

Elements: Emotions: (Human Consciousness), Present: (Time), Information: (Wisdom), No Action: (Choice), Question: (Change), Family: (Worldview), Vicarious: (Memory), Communication: (Human Function), Patterns: (Nature), Self: (Quantum), Content: (Message), Storage: (Data processing sequence), Refuse: (Closed System), Accept: (Open System), Insert: (Transformation).

Sight: Motivator

Based upon what is seen through this sense. Primary Question is Why, (Reasons, Ideas, Concepts) Major Meta: Delete (difference).

Elements: Mental: (Human Consciousness), Past: (Time), Data: (Wisdom), Take Action: (Choice), Direction: (Change), Individual: (Worldview), Real: (Memory), Identity: (Human Function), Structure: (Nature), Wrong: (Quantum), Intent: (Message), Reception: (Data processing sequence), Deny: (Closed System), Admit: (Open System), Delete: (Transformation).

Taste: Reference

Based upon anything experienced by this sense: Primary Question is How. (Belief about character, identifying character), Major Meta: Generalize (difference).

Elements: Physical: (Human Consciousness), Future: (Time), Knowledge: (Wisdom), Let others take action: (Choice), Modeling: (Change), Society: (Worldview), Genetic: (Memory), Creation: (Human Function), Processes: (Nature), Life: (Quantum), Context: (Message), Transmit: (Data processing sequence), Repress: (Closed System), Express: (Open System), Permutation: (Transformation)

Sound: Decision

Based upon anything heard through this sense whether environmental or internal, such as thoughts: Primary Question is What. (Values, Ethics, Meaning) Major Meta: Delete (sameness).

Elements: Mental: (Human Consciousness), Past: (Time), Data: (Wisdom), Take Action: (Choice), Direction: (Change), Individual: (Worldview), Real: (Memory), Identity: (Human Function), Structure: (Nature), Right:

(Quantum), Intent: (Message), Reception: (Data processing sequence), Deny: (Closed System), Admit: (Open System), Delete: (Transformation).

Touch: Motivator

Based upon anything felt through this sense: Primary Question is Who (Relationships, the way things relate with each other), Major Meta: Distort (Amplification).

Elements: Emotions: (Human Consciousness), Present: (Time), Information: (Wisdom), No Action: (Choice), Question: (Change), Family: (Worldview), Vicarious: (Memory), Communication: (Human Function), Patterns: (Nature), God: (Quantum), Content: (Message), Storage: (Data processing sequence), Refuse: (Closed System), Accept: (Open System), Insert: (Transformation).

FUNCTIONIST

Taste: Reference

Based upon anything experienced by this sense: Primary Question is How. (Belief about character, identifying character), Major Meta: Generalize (difference).

Elements: Physical: (Human Consciousness), Future: (Time), Knowledge: (Wisdom), Let others take action: (Choice), Modeling: (Change), Society: (Worldview), Genetic: (Memory), Creation: (Human Function), Processes: (Nature), Life: (Quantum), Context: (Message), Transmit: (Data processing sequence), Repress: (Closed System), Express: (Open System), Permutation: (Transformation).

Sound: Decision

Based upon anything heard through this sense whether environmental or internal, such as thoughts: Primary Question is What. (Values, Ethics, Meaning) Major Meta: Delete (sameness).

Elements: Mental: (Human Consciousness), Past: (Time), Data: (Wisdom), Take Action: (Choice), Direction: (Change), Individual: (Worldview), Real: (Memory), Identity: (Human Function), Structure: (Nature), Right: (Quantum), Intent: (Message), Reception: (Data processing sequence), Deny: (Closed System), Admit: (Open System). Delete: (Transformation).

Touch: Motivator

Based upon anything felt through this sense: Primary Question is Who (Relationships, the way things relate with each other), Major Meta: Distort (Amplification),

Elements: Emotions: (Human Consciousness), Present: (Time), Information: (Wisdom), No Action: (Choice), Question: (Change), Family: (Worldview), Vicarious: (Memory), Communication: (Human Function), Patterns: (Nature), God: (Quantum), Content: (Message), Storage: (Data processing sequence), Refuse: (Closed System), Accept: (Open System), Insert: (Transformation).

Smell: Reference

Based upon what is smelled through this sense. Primary Question is Where. (Strategies) Major Meta: Generalize (sameness),

Elements: Physical: (Human Consciousness), Future: (Time), Knowledge: (Wisdom), Let others take action: (Choice), Modeling: (Change), Society: (Worldview), Genetic: (Memory), Creation: (Human Function), Processes: (Nature), Death: (Quantum), Context: (Message), Transmit: (Data processing sequence), Repress: (Closed System), Express: (Open System), Permutation: (Transformation).

Energy: Decision

Based upon what actions in the environment and within you, also intuitions you have. Primary Question is Which. (Action, Intuition) Major Meta: Distort (diminish).

Elements: Emotions: (Human Consciousness), Present: (Time), Information: (Wisdom), No Action: (Choice), Question: (Change), Family: (Worldview), Vicarious: (Memory), Communication: (Human Function), Patterns: (Nature), Self: (Quantum), Content: (Message), Storage: (Data processing sequence), Refuse: (Closed System), Accept: (Open System), Insert: (Transformation).

Sight: Motivator

Based upon what is seen through this sense. Primary Question is Why, (Reasons, Ideas, Concepts) Major Meta: Delete (difference).

Elements: Mental: (Human Consciousness), Past: (Time), Data: (Wisdom), Take Action: (Choice), Direction: (Change), Individual: (Worldview), Real: (Memory), Identity: (Human Function), Structure: (Nature), Wrong: (Quantum), Intent: (Message), Reception: (Data processing sequence), Deny: (Closed System), Admit: (Open System), Delete: (Transformation).

LIST AT LEAST 7 OF EACH (see pg. 99-100)

    GOAL   DREAM   DESIRE   NEED

CHAPTER 5

THE CAUSE OF CLOSED SYSTEMS

The Cause of Closed Systems

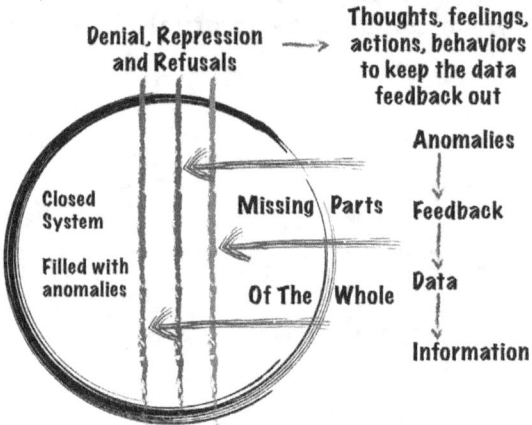

The "Identity" actually burst and the Closed System's "Identity" becomes the very thoughts, feelings, behaviors, perceptions (whole identity) becomes the very boundaries and limits which keeps the anomalies out to keep the System Closed.

Physics of Closed Systems: Addictions

The combined systems of being human when in complete harmony with each other can be an Open system. Open systems are systems that take in feedback, data, from its environment and surroundings and processes these. Humans like other life forms take these in through their senses and have different organs to take this information in.

Humans are Open Systems when operating properly. Conversely, humans can be Closed Systems. Closed Systems do not let new information, data, and feedback come in. Closed systems do not have permeable and flexible boundaries. Closed systems are addictive systems.

Humans are Open Systems and by nature take in Feedback and have Permeable and Flexible boundaries. Open Systems boundaries let all data and feedback enter into the system, much like a sponge and then processes the data and feedback and their boundaries can adjust based on the new learning's and constant growth. This is a natural aspect of this process, this is wisdom, knowledge, progression.

Closed Systems are not open to new Feedback, Data or Information. Success is achieved in Nature through Self-Organization. This is the way the Open System works. This is the way Whole living systems function and grow, just naturally changing with self as a whole based upon the environment and all that's coming into it. When a System becomes Closed, the System as a Whole goes into decline and natural forces come into play. Their only goal is to eliminate or lift the restrictions that keep the System closed. The system's ability to self-organize to its environment can no longer function due to the fact it is no longer able to receive information from the environment.

These natural forces are of the same degree or measure of the system's inability to allow the data and feedback in. Their only purpose is to get the system to open up again to its environment so the system may become Open and Whole and continue to adjust and grow within its surroundings. This is so simple to understand, on the one hand; of course, a human being must continue to adjust and grow within its surrounds. Otherwise, what happens to it?

Stability becomes dysfunctional. A Closed System can only duplicate itself. Repeating the same thing, the same way, every day, every decision, every belief. Never allowing new data or feedback to come into the system. Somewhat of a "my way or the highway" approach. Not only do beliefs not change in a Closed System, thoughts and emotional responses remain the same, time and time again, over and over, increasing in intensity. This is Addiction.

Addicts are anomalies of a Closed System. I know of no one that is a complete Open System. Few people even understand what it means to be an Open System. I will elaborate on this in Chapter 6 to assist you in gaining greater understanding of an Open System.

Addicted people are "other-referent", people not "self-referent". Since so much of themselves has been thrown away from their being Closed that there is little of them left to reference to. Without the feedback and assurance from others, they have very little of their own to rely upon. Closed Systems are made of denial, refusal and repression. In Closed Systems, Identity of an individual, family, or society basis has burst. It is in no sense (innocence).

Anomalies are indicators of an Entropy cycle. Entropy is considered a measure of the unavailable energy in a Closed System that is also usually considered to be the measure of the systems disorder. This is the property of the systems state and will vary directly with any reversible change within the system, to the degree of disorder or uncertainty of a system. Yes, the worldview, the pains and sufferings, the problems in our lives are natural forces coming into play directly related to any reversible change we are capable of.

The function of the entropy is to the ultimate state of inert uniformity; a lacking of the power to move. A deficient in active properties due to the lacking of usual or anticipated actions. Simply put, the entropy (unavailable energy) is unskilled. The entropy releases its available energy in an effort to avoid change due to being unskilled to change itself. We have to recognize our own weaknesses and see the strengths within us to develop our own growth and gain our own greater understandings.

"It is impossible for a man to be saved in ignorance." D&C: 131:6

This is a result of a Closed System, not Open to change, to a point of denying, refusing and repressing any new data from its environment.

Being addicted disowns the spirit. The spirit resides in the space between the central nervous system synapses and surrounds each atom of our being. It is in these spaces of our central nervous system that our atoms correspond with one another to keep us whole. The individual's focus is on its limiting boundaries and barriers that keep it from being an open system. More and more effort is placed on ways to keep new information, data and feedback away from the individual, the family and society. The addict is no longer an individual; it is the boundaries and limits of the Addiction itself. The very behaviors, emotions and thoughts to support the addicted patterns become the person's Identity. Their Identity appears hopeless, depressed, angry, useless, lying, stealing, any and all thoughts, emotions and behaviors supporting the addictive patterns become the individuals Identity. They will make statements regarding their Identity about these boundaries and limits which support their addiction. Statements such as: "I'm hopeless", "I'm depressed", "I'm angry", "I'm sad". I am statements are Identity Level statements. Listen for these "I am", "I'm" statements and you may identify the core beliefs. You may also simply change these "I am"," I'm" statements. You may also create your own "I am", "I'm" statements and repetitively create new Identity (core beliefs). Examples: "I am working on being helpful", "I'm seeking joy". I'm seeking to forgive and be forgiven."

To overcome addiction the individual, family and society must first experience the far from equilibrium states; randomness, complete disorder. This is Nature's way of bringing the System whole again and opening the Closed System.

Research indicates that individuals become addicted in various manners to be able to escape negative emotions, experiences, environments, and other realities for the self. Addictive behaviors result when the item(s) the individual is attempting to escape is inescapable. This must be dealt with and cannot be avoided. The inescapable refers to the True Self and their beliefs. The addiction does not come about based upon the "other references". The addiction is a result of the addict not being "self-referenced" and blaming others. You can run but you cannot hide from yourself.

Anomalies are information that runs counter to the commons (beliefs, norms), These anomalies are actually built into the system from the start. Anomalies deviate from the rules and guidelines turning counter to the whole purpose of the success and other models created. They become so big that they invade and fight the purposes began for. They are frailties and sympathies of the system from the beginning, aspects of the true self which still need to develop and grow. Problems running counter to accomplishing the goal is within the system itself. It is about potential within the system to help the system grow.

Anomalies are inconsistent with or deviating from what is usual, normal, or expected. An anomaly is "uncertain of nature or classification" and is deviating from the norm.

An individual with various talents, gifts and skill is oftentimes prone to attempt to avoid his/her own natural abilities. Becoming discouraged, overwhelmed and other negative perceptions of their life and self, so turn to addictions as a means of avoiding dealing with these false beliefs of themselves.

To be a Closed System, we must deny, refuse or repress the Data and Information available and coming into us from our environment. As an individual or a whole system such as a family or society.

Denial: Refuse to admit the truth, negation of logic, a psychological defense mechanism in which problems or reality, oftentimes even refusing to look at the Data or Information. Ascertaining that an allegation is false becomes a negation in logic. Denial becomes a Psychological defense mechanism in which confrontation with a personal problem or with Reality is avoided by denying the existence of the problem or reality. The Opposite of Deny is Admit.

Refusal: The turning down of a proposal. Rejection, disapproval, refusing to accept internal promptings let alone outside feedback. The act of refusing, rejecting, disapproving and just giving up. The opposite of Refuse is Acceptance.

Repression: Countermeasure, against, revolt. Clamp down, suppression, pacification. The action or processes of repressing: the state of being repressed. A process by which distressing thoughts, memories or impulses that may give rise to anxiety and are excluded from consciousness and left to operate in the subconscious. Put down or prevent Natural development. This is the structure, patterns and processes of a closed system, Addiction.

Being innocent has become unacceptable: Naivety now being considered stupid and unintelligent.

Closed systems are addictive systems, whether individual, family or society. As addicted systems, their problems and crisis is the very feedback from the rest of the system which is being denied, refused, and being repressed any consideration. These feedback loops, themselves, become the anomalies. When addiction takes over, identity has burst. With addiction, we have thrown a part of us out. Nature wants it to fix itself and natural forces are here themselves, to make the system open and whole again.

Anomalies have information that runs counter to common beliefs and norms. Still, it is information and should not be ignored.

Anomalies challenge the system. They are defects and flaws that were built unconsciously into the system (individual, family or society) in the beginning. Anomalies are deviations of the rules, standards and beliefs.

When anomalies go too far, they appear as violations and abuses until they actually create or cause the far from equilibrium states in the individual, family, or society. Withdrawal for the addict brings this state and can lead to the addict choosing to not use the drug or alcohol again. Then becoming an Open System. Addicts are other-referenced people and not self-referent. The addict requires this outside feedback in order to break through his/her own barriers and find their self again. You are the outside force to help the addict become whole again. Anomalies are beneficial.

ASSIGNMENT for Chapter 5

From the lists you completed in Chapter 4, the list of your Desires, Goals, Dreams and Needs, choose the ones from each list that you attained, or you're working on. Place them on a separate piece of paper under their appropriate category and list the others on the 4 separate pages in their category.

Under each Desire, Goal, Dream and Need list 1 of each of the 3 things identified on the page. You are to give good consideration to this assignment.

It asks that you think of and write for each at least: 1 Event, 1 Condition and 1 process you know or believe it will take to accomplish and or fulfill each. Example"

Desire -: 1): To restore an old car.

List to fulfill this:

a). Event: Obtain an old car to restore.
b). Condition: Your state of being mental, emotional and physical needed.
c). Process: Plan for doing it
d). Date:

It may help to think of others you may know or have heard about who have these already and know or imagine the Events, Conditions and Processes they might have gone through to get to where they are today regarding the Desire, Goal, Dream or Need. Find a Role Model or imagine one and identify or imagine the patterns they used.

This process is very important. Take your time doing this and look at a way of doing this assignment from an objective point of view. Considering another's perceptions and experiences may help you come up with your list.

Schedule 3 different times per each Desire, Goal, Dream and Need that you will do the Event, while having the Condition and doing the Process you choose, over the next 12 months to complete your entire list of all 28 you have listed.

You may do 1 of each on a Future Memory guided imagery.

CHAPTER 6

OPEN SYSTEMS

Living Systems are Open Systems; Open Systems take in Feedback, Data, and Energy from its environment. Open Systems have different Modalities to receive the input from the environment, simply due to the fact that all its possible areas of the input are Open and not Closed to the input. Take a nail and try to hammer it into cement. It takes a special nail gun to get the cement to allow the nail to penetrate it. Take a nail and try to hammer it into a piece of wood. Not only does it go into the wood, the wood changes some of its shape inside and out to allow the nail to penetrate it. Things of nature must be Open Systems, or they will die. A tree, a plant, even the seed and root must be open. If any of these have boundaries which are not permeable and flexible the tree or plant will die, if the seed or root is closed the plant or tree cannot even grow. The plant can adjust by itself to the environment in numerous ways to assure its survival. This is Self-organizing.

An Open System is a Whole System. Its Disorder is Discontinuous because it is constantly taking in new Data, Corresponding and Integrating the new Data into its current Models, Programs and Processes.

The three main Functions of being an Open System are:

1) Admit the continual Data from the environment
2) Accept the Data, dialogue the Data. Experience the Dialogue of the Data. Create New Theories of the new Data, Dialogue and Experiences

3) Express the new Knowledge and Discernments from the Awareness of the new Data. Implementing the new theories of the dialogue of the new data and be open to its feedback

a) Admit Open Systems Believe the Data coming into the system to the point of Acknowledging the Data, they do not consider it delusional, unreal nor surreal. It Admits and Affirms the Data as having a purpose. It allows the Data to go through the Open Systems for processing anything of importance. Open Systems "Own" the Data coming into it. This means it Believes, Affirms, Admits, and Acknowledges it.
b) Accepting the Data includes the processing of the Data in the Open System. The processing is done without a judgment or reaction. Permitting acceptance of all the Data to be processed, dialogued and New Theories looked at without Protest or Reaction.
c) Open Systems having acquired and experienced this new Data,

Express their new Learning's vigorously and emotionally through their Actions and Communications. Open Systems give voice to their New Awareness. Socially and Intellectually due to the Anomalies and Feedback that is all a part of our Living Cycle, our Being. This allows any data from the environment to be used to improve the system. No environmental feedback can throw an open system into decline when it maintains itself open. An Open System does not feel a need to try to control the feedback, it is not intimidated or anxious or depressed due to the data and feedback.

An Open System is continually growing (flexible boundaries) from life experiences. It isn't denying, refusing and repressing the data and feedback from its environment (permeability).

This process is continuous in all aspects of our life and it cycles through these three Patterns to maintain an Open System. Open Systems process the Disorder from its environment and the Disorder is naturally Discontinuous Disorder because the system constantly grows.

When the body's feedback is denied, repressed or rejected, the body does not heal itself and the problem whether physical, mental or emotional, stays chronic. Withdrawal from drugs or alcohol is a good example of this process. When the body cramps, vomits or experiences diarrhea, withdrawal symptoms begins. It's the body's process of getting the toxins out of the body systems. When other medications are given to stop the body's process towards wholeness again, the problem remains in a chronic stage.

In order to attain a state of Wholeness or Health, the individual, family, society, must go through the acute stage to get to Health and Wholeness. Once in the Health or Wholeness state again, natural anomalies appear, and once again we go through another acute state to deal with the chronic (anomalies) state to return to the Health and Wholeness. Repeat, repeat, repeat. There is no cure for life's problems whether individual or global. There are, however, natural processes built into each human individual for growth because of life's problems. Whether they belong to us as individuals or to the world, there are natural ways to overcome and grow. Natural body functions, internal processes and models for overcoming and growing. We see this in nature with forest fires and new growth.

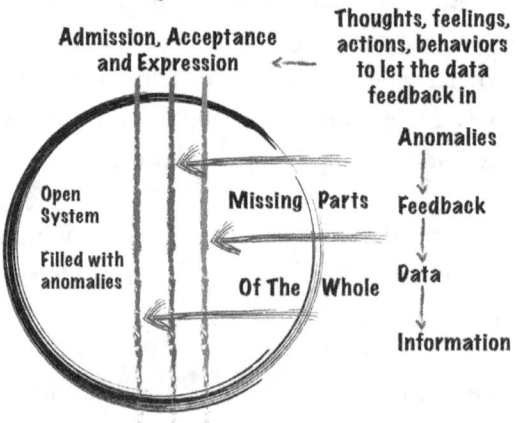

Disorder becomes discontinuous and "Identity" becomes ever changing and unpredictable.

Idealist Open System

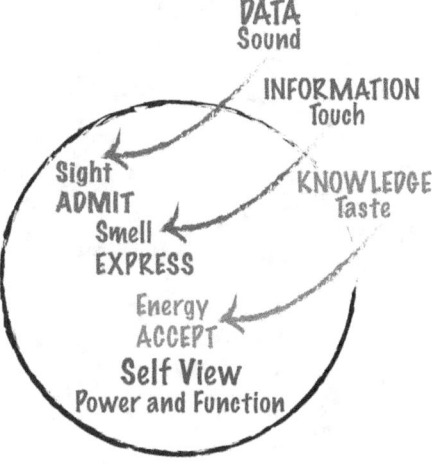

Conceptualist Open System

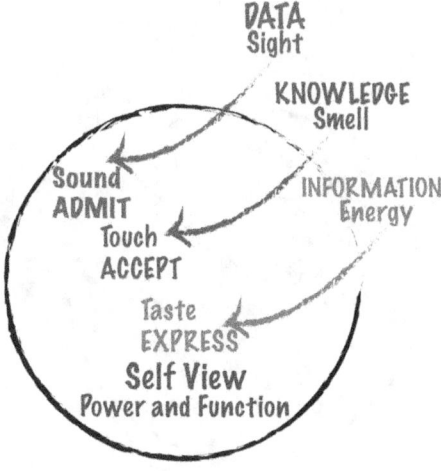

Relationalist Open System

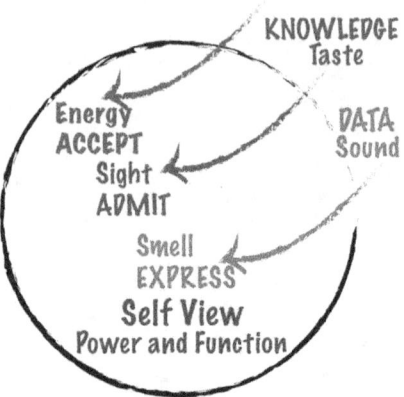

Actionist Open System

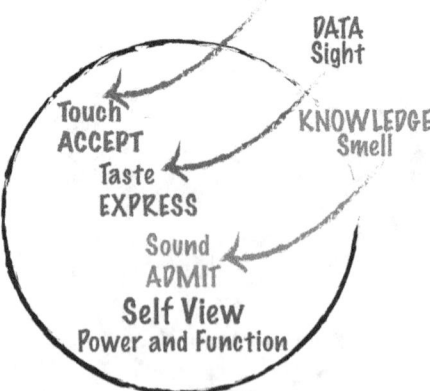

Functionist Open System

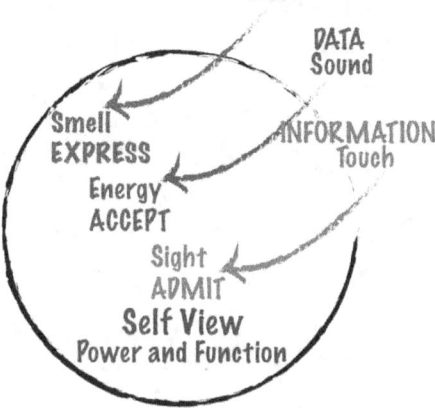

Strategist Open System

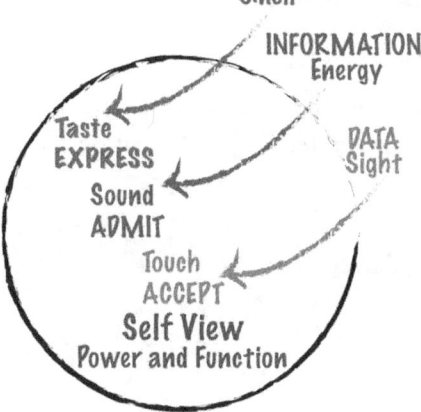

OPEN SYSTEM TECHNIQUE

Place a circle on the floor. Identify 3 locations both along the outside and inside of the circle.

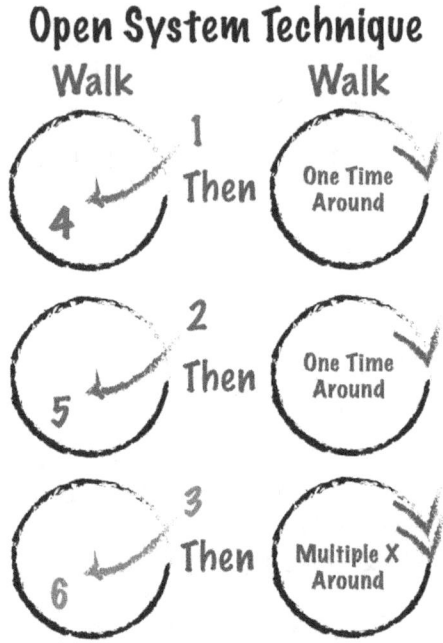

Final Step: Walk around circle 7 times or until a shift occurs. Then, step into circle and make an "I AM" statement.

Start on the locations on the outside of the circle and walk from 1 to 4 answering the questions stated for each location based upon your sensory firing order.

Technique Walking Pattern: 1 to 4
                                                                       2 to 5
                                                                       3 to 6

When this process is completed you will have walked your 1st sense to your 4th sense, answering each question for each sense. Then, walk the circle one time. Then, step on to your 2nd sense and walk it to your 5th sense, answering each question for each sense. Then, walk the circle one time. Then, step on to your 3rd sense and walk it to your 6th sense, answering each question for each sense. Then, continue to walk the circle repetitively at least 7 times or until you sense a neurological shift. Then step into the center of the circle and state an "I Am" _____ Statement.

Questions for Open System Technique for different Sensory Personalities:

Conceptualist

1. Why did this data come to you (me)?
4. What can I gain in direction from this data?
2. Where does the information in the feedback lead me?
5. Who is here to assist my answers in my life now?
3. Which intuition or action does this feedback reflect about me?
6. How may I use this to gain knowledge and express myself greater?

Idealist

1. What of this data is about my past?
4. Why do I reason and justify about it so (as I do)?
2. Who is attempting to inform me of something?
5. Where may it help me organize and attain my future?
3. How is this knowledge for my future?
6. Which actions and intuitions do I have that currently block this information and knowledge?

Relationalist

1. Whose relationships if this about now?
4. Which action/intuition of mine, now, may gain new theories from it?
2. How is the knowledge expressed that's important to me?
5. Why is any data in that of reason for me to see?
3. What value did the data have in my life's direction?
6. Where might I know, what might I rearrange to better express my knowledge?

Actionist

1. Which action or intuition do I refuse and accept?
4. Who do these mostly accept in my life?
2. Why did things appear like that?
5. How might I rearrange my processes to gain greater knowledge from those?
3. Where is any importance in this and what model might it represent?
6. What values might I be denying of myself that relate to this?

Strategist

1. Where is any importance and knowledge for me in this?
4. How may I process or model to rearrange for knowledge in this?
2. Which action and intuition do I currently refuse about this information?
5. What value or meaning of my past might I be denying this might be about?
3. Why do I see that, are there parts I deny seeing or reasons I deny about it?
6. Who in my present might I question about and look at new theories about in my relationships currently?

Functionist

1. How may I process or model to rearrange for knowledge in this?
4. Where is any importance and knowledge for me in this?
2. What value or meaning of my past might I be denying this might be about?
5. Which action and intuition do I currently refuse about this information?
3. Who in my present might I question about and look at new theories about in my relationships currently?
6. Why do I see that, are there parts I deny seeing or reasons I deny about it?

CHAPTER 7

TIME AND ADDICTIONS

Addictive systems; Systems that are closed to natural forms of feedback from the environment become Addictive systems. This is when one or more of the systems have plummeted on other parts of the system resulting in the process not being completed. Addictions, whether drugs, alcohol, negative thoughts, feelings, behaviors, all have Time Lines they can't disassociate from. In order to change the addiction, they must be disassociated from the Time Line event(s) and or emotion(s) controlling the addiction(s). Events which have caused them pain, suffering from their past and clinging to them and keeping them stuck in their past and oftentimes afraid of their future. We were born open systems our life's struggles that we do not overcome and grow from bury us turning us into closed systems. Again, this is all about the strengths we have inside of ourselves that we have not yet recognized and trained for our growth. Being able to "watch" Time is through time. Seeing Time from the past to the future; watching through Time, assists in evaluating consequences, cause and effects. People that cannot see through time, cannot imagine, and cannot see the consequences of their choices and behaviors. This is an "Objective" perception of our time and the experiences in our time. Through Time, people are evaluative individuals.

People stuck in Time, can't get out of pain or problems. When we have experiences, thoughts or emotions that continue to be foremost in our memories, we get stuck in the time of these memories. The memory doesn't have to have conscious detailed memory; simply the emotion brought about by the memory can hold our life captive to the time of the memory. In the subconscious, a memory is just an event, the details are not necessarily directly tied into the same program model or part of the brain as the event is. The details are sought out by the brain when the event is pulled into conscious and if you are thinking of an event, it is pulled into your conscious. Oftentimes, we get stuck in our Past time and in the subconscious we are experiencing our present and our future from the past memories stored in the subconscious. This makes it virtually impossible to actually experience our present moments or even imagine a future to be much different than the past we are stuck in. These individuals, stuck in Time, get involved in drugs or alcohol or other addictive thoughts and behaviors that are self-limiting of growth and change.

All things done within our bodies are for a positive intent. Disease, discomfort, emotion, behavior or thought are all things the subconscious control for a state of Wholeness for the individual. Pain, for example, has the positive intent of notifying the conscious mind that something is wrong. The body knows what is needed for it to be healthy, mentally, emotionally and physically and works diligently to communicate this to us, sometimes through a very challenging process. Getting our attention to what the body is telling us is a great challenge to our whole being. Our body even in disease is attempting to make itself better to a state of Wholeness.

Changing to a state of Wholeness does not stop an individual from being able to experience or do the negative thing. It allows for the individual to choose to do the negative thing or to choose to do the positive thing. In order to choose to not do anything, there must be a positive thing to choose to do. CHOICE is the ultimate purpose, not control.

Time Line Orientation

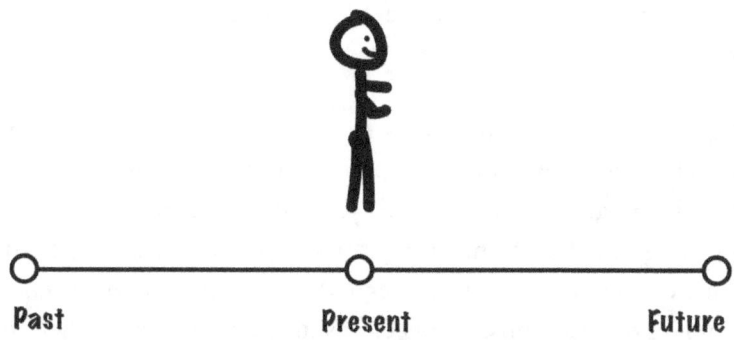

A normal Time Line with Past Behind and Future in Front.

Switched Time Line Orientation

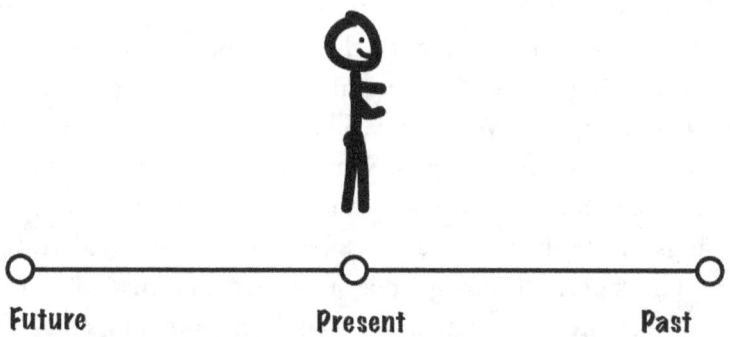

A Time Line with Past in Front, and Future Behind. Many people with addictive patterns repeat the past and may have this orientation.

Future Guided Imagery

Introduction:

I've heard it said that we weave our future in our present, with the memories from our past. Hopefully you're doing some past time line work. Sometimes past memory work is as simple as talking to other human beings about our past life experiences. There are a lot of other ways available to work with our past.

Working with our past memories is extremely important. As human beings, to be able to overcome our past, we must learn how to talk about it, how to think about our past, how to perceive our past. We are also as human beings constantly having future memories, and we usually call these future memories hopes or dreams, goals, things that we choose or desire to have or accomplish. This CD is intended to assist in helping you get conscious and subconscious support in having, in hoping, in achieving your futures. Please place yourself in a comfortable position, make sure you have 20 minutes or half an hour to listen to this CD.

Future Guided Imagery Dialogue:

"Close your eyes and take three deep cleansing breaths in through your nose and out through your mouth. Breathe normally again and relax. Imagine something incredible, something that you have always dreamed of having or doing, or even being. Something that is just so exciting, overwhelming, encompassing you. Something in your future, something incredible. Something that would bring you more joy, more of all of the good things in life than you can possibly imagine. A wonderful future memory. Think of this future memory in great detail. In all of its glorious aspects and pleasures, be it something big or be it something small. Choose something now, that you're having it fulfills some part of you. And with this thought in your mind, imagine floating right out of your body, or imagine a bird's eye view of yourself as you are positioned now. Safely and comfortably and securely, floating above, a bird's eye view of where you are, and with this future goal, dream or desire in your mind, float along all of your future memories, and pick an ideal spot for you to have this future memory. And when you are at the ideal spot in your future memories, ... find an ideal location for the memory in front of you as you are position above your future memories, your bird's eye view of your future, and this memory begins to create itself in any way you can imagine it being created, whether it is real life, whether it is on a movie screen, in any way that you can imagine or pretend to imagine, watch this future memory develop in its fullness right in front of you as you are positioned above your future memories. Watch this memory become moving, living, breathing, notice all of the human sensory experiences as you watch this memory out in front of you. Notice all of the environment in this memory, all of the panoramic views of this memory.

And imagine that you have in your possession positioned here above your future memories, watching, observing this future memory, that you have a control panel, and with this control panel you can make any and all of the adjustments that you choose to make in this memory as you observe it. You can change color and sound, texture smell and taste, you can change depth and dimension, time, and you can choose to make all the adjustments that you choose to make. In order to have this future memory perfect for you. And when you have made all of the adjustments that you choose to make on this future memory, imagine, or pretend to imagine, safely, comfortably, and securely from your bird's eye view, stepping right into all of this memory. Experiencing now all of the sights and sounds, the smells and tastes, the temperatures and textures, the energies and intuitions, the sense of yourself in this memory. And imagine, that you have here too a panel to make all the adjustments that you may choose to have this memory even more, even better, than you'd ever imagined it.

And notice how you feel in this memory, notice your conscious thoughts in this memory. Notice your feelings and sensations in this memory. Notice what others may be thinking and feeling with you in this memory, Notice all of the aspects of anyone and anything and the experience of it, in this memory, and make any and all adjustments that you choose to make to have this memory be everything you can possibly imagine. And when this memory is perfect for you and for others, imagine or pretend to imagine that you safely and securely step out of this memory and float, and have you bird's eye view of all of your future memories, and again observing this future memory out in front of you, watching it again, in detail. Making sure, And when this memory is everything that you choose to have this memory be, imagine, floating this future memory right down into the position that you have chosen on your future timeline, this memory being placed now on your future timeline exactly where you choose to place it with your future memories, and in any way that you imagine, or pretend to imagine, secure this future memory onto your future memory timeline. And floating back above your future timeline or experiencing your bird's eye view of your future memories, notice anything and everything that may be different now, on your future memory timeline, having placed this memory in your future timeline. Notice any changed in color, in brightness or length or width or dimension or texture or hues, anything and everything that may look different in your future memory timeline, now, and notice from your bird's eye view, you positioned there in you now, and notice anything that may seem different as you observe you there in your now, having placed this future memory in your future memory timeline. And notice the power you have in your minds, the control you have in your minds to change your futures. To have, to be, whatever you choose to have or to be, in your future. Floating back now, to you in your present, changing your bird's eye view from your future to you in your present, and floating right down into yourself again, knowing the things that are there for you in your future, knowing the power of your minds, knowing the textures, the colors, the sounds, the smells, the tastes, the intuitions and energies, knowing you in that future memory. You in your now, you who has the power, you who controls your future from your very now. Breathing deeper, feeling more body sensation, being aware of things in your current present, now environment, feeling relaxed and alert, feeling in charge and confident, open your eyes."

Thank you.

End of dialogue.

Each body system is intended to be an Open System and part of the whole system (Wholeness), which is a whole system (Totality), when all systems are Open and Corresponding together, we have the Whole system's (Identity). When any system is closed, in any area another body system is plummeted into by the closed area's system. This plummet literally means that all the body systems and senses functions, processes and purpose is imposed upon another body system to carry out for the closed system. This is the way one body organ begins to break down (closed system) and other organs and body systems begin to be negatively affected by the organ or system closing down. This is the body system's attempt to get Wholeness back. When it plummets into another system, Identity is lost. The system which is closed has lost identity and the system plummeting into the closed system loses its identity by taking on the other systems functions. Our inner enemy is the Self, plummeting us, to open our system up. This then becomes the addicted process; the Closed System. When it plummets, it plummets to the Corresponding body system as illustrated on the following body map. The Closed system can also be identified with linguistics, by the word(s) used to describe the problem you or another individual has.

Each human sense has its own identity, function and elements. When any sensory system is closed another sensory system must pick up the identity, functions and elements of the closed sensory system. For example, the sense of Sight's Identity is for us to see. The subconscious takes all we see through our sense of sight and creates programs for our Ideas, Reasons and Concepts, the element of Past, Data, Take action, and many other elements are programmed in our subconscious from the sense of sight. If then, the sense of Smell gets closed and plummets into the sense of sight, sight must also do all the function and elements smell should be doing.

Smell's function is to create programs for strategies in the subconscious and some elements associated with the sense of smell are Future, Knowledge and letting others to take action.

Sight being ideas, reasons and concepts, our past, data, and take action doing also the subconscious processes for smell of strategies, our future, knowledge, and letting others take action means this conscious experience: strategies for our future are based on past ideas, reasons and concepts: Knowledge is based upon data only with no information involved and letting others take action is only accomplished by taking action ourselves. All of these closed system areas cause the whole system to be dysfunctional resulting in self-view patterns of cycling through its dysfunctional program models. Round and around and around you go and how you got here no one knows. (But you).

These are the subconscious structures, patterns and processes just based upon the nature of the subconscious functions. This happens to every human being and is a subconscious program with a devastating conscious effect on our abilities to change, no matter how much we want to.

ILLUSTRATION OF THE HOLOGRAPHIC HUMAN BODY MAP AND THE SENSORY BODY LOCATION WITH EACH SCORE FROM THE EVALUATION IN CHAPTER ONE - AND WHAT'S LOST DEPENDING ON THE SYSTEM THAT IS NOT COMPLETELY OPEN AND WHAT HAPPENS TO THAT PART OF THE PERSON. Sound- values, meaning, past. Sight- ideas, reason, past. Touch- relationships, present. Energy- actions, present. Taste- beliefs of character of self and ability to judge another's character, future. Smell- beliefs of strategies, future.

Study this map and learn to identify in yourself the sensory areas that are closed in your subconscious and begin to learn to understand your own conscious experience, based upon the subconscious processes.

Referring to the Holographic Human Map with the "Q" and "A" and the number to the question or answer listed in that area of the map is the area of the Question and Answer from the test in Chapter 2. This lets you identify the sense and their functions either working or not working. This map illustration reference applies only to the questions and answers from the questionnaire, which indicates a Closed sense.

Sound
What?
Values, Ethics and Meanings

Sight
Why?
Ideas, Reasons and Concepts

Touch
Who?
Relationships

Time/
Self
When?

Energy
Which?
Intuitions

Taste
How?
Beliefs about character

Smell
Where?
Beliefs about how things work

Human Paradigm Map

Right Side
Q5 A1
Q6 A1
Q8 A2
Q9 A-A
Q10 A3
Q11 A-A

Left Side
Q5 A1
Q6 A1
Q8 A2
Q9 A-A
Q10 A3
Q11 A-A

Q5 A2   Q1
Q6 A4   Q3
Q8 A3
Q9 A-B
Q10 A2
Q11 A-B

Q5 A2   Q3
Q6 A4
Q8 A3
Q9 A-B
Q10 A2
Q11 A-B

Q1
Q2
Q4
Q5 A3
Q6 A2
Q8 A4
Q9 A-C
Q10 A1
Q11 A-C

Q1
Q2
Q4
Q5 A3
Q6 A2
Q7
Q8 A4
Q9 A-C
Q10 A1   Q11 A-C

OC Questionnaire Map

Use this page to document the senses you are Closed in based upon this Holographic Human Map referenced with the Questions and Answers.

Closed Senses and their function and elements:

Use this page to write the consequences or effects of these senses being closed based upon the sensory function and its elements along with the sense it plummeted to and the resulting combination of overload on the plummeting sense.

Describe and explain your own conscious experience because of these senses being closed.

Use this space to list the senses that you are Open in based upon the questionnaire and the questions and answers NOT on the illustrated map.

Use this page to describe the conscious effects of theses senses being Open, the functions and elements that your conscious and subconscious does have access to.

SYSTEM ASSIGNMENT FORM

Each day you interact with the addict fill out this form for your own education. (Educate: to draw out), again your own wisdom is already within you. Remember, the addict has greater talents, abilities and even beliefs within them regarding themselves, their World View and their Self View.

With this in mind as you observe and interact consider ways to "educate" both yourself and the addict regarding these in them.

No one is a complete Open System though the more you practice being an Open System the more open you may become.

1) Admit–

What did you hear them say?

What did you see them do or what did they tell you they did?

2) Accept–

Write a dialogue, a synopsis based upon what you heard and saw. Write theories (plans) of ways to approach them to assist or help them. Incorporate (plans to) these theories and be open to additional data and feedback from them in their responses (this is Admit again, step 1 of an Open System)

3) Express–

Do the plan you created in Accept step 2 and repeat this plan for 3-7 days repeating Admit in step 1 and write a dialogue a synopsis of anything you yourself are learning through this process. Keep a journal about all you learn about yourself, the other person, and life in general. You may begin here.

CHAPTER 8

UNBRIDGEABILITY

Unbridgeability is about choices, choice is a quantum leap syndrome. Be willing to let go to be one with self and God and move to your goals, nurture yourself when others are not willing to choose to go with you, they choose to stay.

Mind, emotions (spirit) and body have two quantum leaps each:

QUANTUMS

1. Right
2. God
3. Life

4. Wrong
5. Self
6. Death

Choice of the first three implies choice of the last three quantum. You cannot have one without the other. There must be opposition in all things. Each opposite is associated with its opposing element. These quantum's are a part of the subconscious programming we are born with. We have an inner sense of right and wrong and the other quantum. They each have their own identity, function, elements, and one does not become the other. Still, they do inter-relate inter-dependently and are integers to one another. Resistance occurs when the associated Quantum changes (rest of set) and is not bridgeable. As human beings we cannot have a life without a death being a natural part of the life. We cannot be a self without having God a natural part of us. We cannot do right without a wrong being a natural aspect of this.

When these quantum's leap back and forth, resistance occurs between the opposing quantum. Such as, a mental defensive response to the opposing quantum, as though the opposing quantum is a resistive force. When in reality it is not. In reality, we, as human beings have not yet learned to take opposition in all things and turn them into something which may be passed through or over. The bridging of the quantum's makes these passable, navigable, and negotiable.

Right is not wrong nor is wrong ever right. Just as with any element with its own identity, respect for the individual identity of each is imperative. Having the awareness of the bridgeability of these opposing quantum's opens our inner sense of these to naturally access the passages and directions from the one to the other. Man's wisdom has taught so many principles which have taken mankind far away from the simple truths. Simple truths then, to a point, seem senseless to mankind's intellect and wisdom.

God sent us here with all we need, and this does not just refer to earth, air, and water. Even within our own mind and soul, is our knowledge we came to earth with. Just as one day we may leave this earth with the knowledge we have gained here; we came with knowledge. Man has done and accomplished many great achievements, though none will ever surpass the ability within each human being.

When we can learn to recognize or maybe even just remember the identity, function and elements of each quantum, we also gain a greater sense of these within our daily life's experience. Often times, just the awareness of, may be a great asset when repeated in our conscious mind.

So often in our lives, we question our own sense of right and wrong, God and self, and life and death. We know these as the individual identities they have always been. Man has made many attempts to explain the relationship of these and they are not explained by stating that they are one, or there is no difference between them, or any other explanation. They are opposite of each other, they are real. They have individual, separate identities, functions, and elements which comprise each. In Holographic Human Theory, each Identity remains itself even though they may inter-relate, interdependently, and correspond with other identities.

Quantum's become bridgeable through this very process, of corresponding, interdependently interrelated with each other. Just as relationships, such as a family: The father and mother and children maintain their own identity, one does not just become the other. When one must become the other due to a lack of the other, the one taking on two roles may go into an overload at times.

Bridging the quantum's will never be accomplished in a Closed System. The system must be and remain Open in order for quantum's to be able to correspond as they are capable of doing and to help us be whole.

When all Quantum states become bridgeable, Quantum leaps dissolve and Awareness of Unity occurs. Awareness of Unity is a conscious knowledge of the Identity and Element of something and an ability to observe from your experiences through direct or intuitive perception intangible states or qualities. This knowledge and intuition of the intangible regards the functions, origins, cause and connections with what is needed for oneness. The ability to know the origins or deviations, causes, motives and reason, the Identities and Elements to bring continuity without the deviations (anomalies).

Being naturally, consciously aware of life's potential deviations prior to their actual appearance in your life. Awareness of Unity brings a condition of harmony, continuity without deviation or change in your goal and purpose.

Quantum's leap between the third and fourth sensory firings, as the details of the ways of dealing with the anomalies showing up in the third sense fired brings about the same effect, leaping back and forth, trying to turn one into the other. The Transformation change process of Bridgability keeps the senses from closing and keeps Identity growing and progressing successfully.

Know Thy Self

Then

Heal Thy Self

Know and Heal Others

As the Quantum's pertain to Open & Closed Systems: Know Thy Self pertains to our choice of Right and Wrong and Taking Action. Heal Thy Self pertains to our choice of God and Self and Take No Action. Know and Heal Others pertains to our choice of Life and Death and Letting Others Take Action. A Closed System will never Know Itself, nor Heal Itself, nor Know and Heal Another.

1) KNOW THY SELF
2) HEAL THY SELF
3) KNOW AND HEAL OTHERS

This process must happen before we can truly Know Others then Heal Others. As Jesus said we must first take the mote out of our own eye before we can take out of another's eye.

One person does not an addict, alcoholic make. It took a team to get us here and it takes a team to get us out and keep us out. This team is family. Family is the way we are created. Whether married or single it still took a male and a female to create a child. This, we call family.

Education is important for children and adults. The dictionary defines educate as to draw out. The family should be drawing out aspects of each individual. Qualities, abilities, talents, family should have a sense of commonality between the members and in the family environment. The family model of unity and security in their environment is the same model the individuals will use in society. Once the individuals know their talents and abilities, they learn to harmonize them in the family environment for a sense of balance. The environment includes the body's responses and reactions to different thoughts, feelings, and behaviors.

This environmental response is reflective of the external environment the individual has been trained to respond to in. The subconscious codes things by where we think about them. This applies to the Body Map and other trigger points of memories, programs, processes, and models.

Children will reflect back or mirror to their parents, other siblings, the family, community, areas the parents and others in their environment are denying. These denials can be about suppressed need, denied need, rejected needs, talents, drives. The beliefs that have been hidden within and violated by the person's patterns created to avoid their pains and sufferings. Addiction violates our own true believing; all it takes to keep the addiction going becomes antagonistic to the true beliefs.

The Scriptures state "the sins of the parents are on the heads of the children for 4 generations".

We must change ourselves before we may assist another to change. In order to change one's self, one must first know one's self. Even though you might think that you do know yourself, if you have personal problems you cannot overcome, if you have personal goals you keep striving for that you cannot attain, then you do not truly know yourself. I believe that we do not have problems that we cannot overcome. I believe that if we have a goal we strive for, we also have the means and abilities to attain the goal.

An excellent way to truly know yourself is to know your inner self, your subconscious self. Just knowing yourself consciously only, and yet still not overcome or attain what your conscious knows; get to know you subconscious self and you can then consciously overcome your problems better. Then you may consciously attain your conscious goals. Conscious can override subconscious. First conscious must know the subconscious programs that are running.

CHAPTER 8 ASSIGNMENT

LIST YOUR MAIN (MAJOR) MEMORIES OF YOUR PAST, LIST WHERE YOU THINK YOU ARE IN YOUR PRESENT, LIST YOUR MAIN (MAJOR) GOALS (MEMORIES) OF YOUR FUTURE.

Past Major Memories

Present Placement

Future Major Memories

CHAPTER 9

MEMORY AND ADDICTIONS

Memory plays a Major role in the development of our Personality, Identity, Communication processes and our Core Beliefs. The Subconscious takes Data from our Sensory experiences and processes these for the Conscious part of our brain to Perceive, Evaluate, Judge and Decide about. These Conscious responses are then taken by the Subconscious and processed and thus, we end up with thought patterns, emotional responses, behavioral patterns and Core Beliefs.

We call these Models and Programs our Identity, Personality, and our whole life's experiences can end up being based just on this process alone, not considering providence and interventions from others. Not just the Sensory experience, but the Conscious Perception of the experience plays a large role in the Models and Programs resulting from the experience. The way you actually perceive your life events and experiences has a greater impact on your subconscious (program/model) than the experience itself. It is very true to look for the good, to look for the lessons to learn, to forgive and see life's challenges as opportunity to grow. Your conscious perception is the master of the programs from your life experiences. If you see you being picked on, put down, not capable, not smart enough, or not good enough, and if this is your conscious perception, then this is the symbol and bulk of the program.

These memories build over a period of time and everyone ends up eventually having negative, even hurtful Sensory experiences. Negative, even harmful Conscious responses can result in negative even harmful Models and Programs. This process develops dysfunctional Models and Programs which everyone has to some degree.

Even though much of the Sensory data in the Subconscious processes come from the environment, the Subconscious through its Data Compression Programs, takes the data with the Conscious response, and by the time we are about 8 years old, the Conscious responses themselves end up being a Model and Program already created by us. We are programmed in what we perceive the way we evaluate and judge and make our decisions.

Memory is used by the Subconscious to create the way we experience the Present and the way we will experience the Future. There is a Native American saying, "We create our Future, in the Present, with the fabric of our Past."

Memory is a Totality and consists of 3 separate Elements each having a separate Function.

Elements of Memory:

Real

Vicarious

Genetic

"Real" Memory is used by the Subconscious to create our Identity and our Personality. "Real" Memory is stored as "Past" Memory, so ends up being the foundation which creates our "Present" experiences Conscious Perceptions, evaluations, judgments and decisions.

"Vicarious" Memory is used by the Subconscious to create our Emotional response and our Communication processes. "Vicarious" Memory is stored as "Present" Memory and is the foundation we have to build our "Future".

"Genetic" Memory is used by the Subconscious to create our Core Beliefs of self, functions, strategies. "Genetic" Memory is literally memory from our lineage, our ancestry; this comes in physical, mental, character traits. Genetic Memory does give us a great opportunity in that it is memory of Events without all the conscious responses of the event. This gives the individual containing the memory the opportunity to perceive, evaluate, judge and decide for ourselves the conscious perception, interpretation and use of the event memory. Again, it is the conscious response to the event, experience that commands the subconscious (unconscious), belief of the program model.

Memories play a large role in Addiction both for the addict and their loved ones. You can't just "get over something". You can't just "go around it" or "go under it". You must go through it. You must learn and grow from it.

Memory itself ends up being just Programmed-Models created in the Subconscious. The "Past", "Present", and "Future", just repetition of the same over and over.

You must literally go back to the "Past" Memories which are negative and maybe even harmful and learn from them to change your "Present". Changing your "Present" is the only way to change your, yes, you get it, your "Future".

You literally create your "Future" every moment with every conscious thought you have in response to every bit of data coming into your conscious from your subconscious. Take conscious control over this process and create your own "Future", the way you would choose to have it be.

There are guided imageries to help you both deal with the "Past" and create the "Future". You can also learn to do this process as an Experiential Guided Imagery.

Past Guided Imagery

Introduction:

The subconscious stores all of our information, sensory based information, whatever other kinds of information may be available to us, it stores it on a timeline. There is only one way in which the subconscious in its processing of information in the subconscious will stop processing information. The subconscious will stop processing information stored in the subconscious when, and only when, conscious has made decisions and judgments about the information in the subconscious. Then and only then will the subconscious stop processing information when conscious has made conscious judgment and choices, perceptions on a conscious level about the subconscious information. This is one of the reasons that dealing with our past is so very, very important. Until and unless we deal completely with all of our deeper past, our subconscious will continue to process that information with all of the other information in our present and even into our future dreams and goals. I'm sure that each and every one of us have memories from our past that have repeated themselves in our present, that we worry may repeat themselves in our future. We are about to do a little guided imagery to do some work to clean up our past timeline.

Place yourself in a comfortable position, where you can have a few moments, perhaps 20 or 30 minutes of quiet to listen to this CD. Determine in your conscious mind the situation from your past, perhaps you don't know the situation so it can just be an experience from your present. It can be an emotion that you are consciously choosing not to have anymore. That you consciously are aware of that you experience in your present.

Determine and write down the thing that you have decided to work on in doing some work on your past to clean it up so that your subconscious can put it away, so that your now's and your futures will no longer be brought down by your past.

Past Guided Imagery Dialogue:

Being comfortable, please take three deep cleansing breaths, in through your nose and out through your mouth. And imagine, just imagine, you can even just pretend to imagine. Imagine that you can float right out of your body now or pretend to imagine a bird's eye view of yourself just as you are positioned right now. And from your safe floating or bird's eye view position, looking at yourself positioned from your bird's eye view or from your safe and secure floating view, imagine or pretend to imagine floating, safely, securely, with your bird's eye view above all of your past memories, your life before now. And imagine, floating along, looking down on your timeline, until you come to the spot that appears or seems to be the place on your timeline, where the thing that you wrote down, to deal with and remove from your past is located. Remaining above your past memories, looking down, bird's eye view of your past, notice color, notice depth, notice texture, dimension, lightness and brightness and length. And while remaining above your timeline, imagine in any way that you choose to imagine that this memory is released from your timeline, and on a guiding wire of some sort, ascends to your safe and secure position above your timeline. And allowing this memory to float out in front of your where you can observe it from a safe distance.

Notice this memory from your safe, bird's eye view, from your secure floating position, notice all of the details of this memory, notice everyone and everything in this memory, notice the sounds, the smells and the tastes and the textures, the energies, the intuitions in this memory, not only of your own remembrance, but also notice the remembrance of others in this memory. Observing all the details of this memory, from your safe position floating above your past line with this memory ascended in front of you, balanced in the air in front of you.

Imagine in any way that you choose to imagine or pretend to imagine, that you can absorb everything of value from everyone and everything in this memory. You can imagine or pretend to imagine that simply by looking and watching, observing, listening to this memory as it floats in front of you, that simply by observing it, you can absorb all of the lessons that each and every person and thing could have, should have, might-ought to have learned from this experience. Or you can imagine or pretend to imagine that simply by holding your hand out toward this memory that you may absorb all of the beneficial lessons and wisdoms that could have, should have, might ought to have been learned from each and every person and thing in this memory, and imagine, or just pretend to imagine, that all of these wisdoms, all of these lessons, all of that learning is absorbed through your perception and observing now, through your gesture of holding your hand, now, toward this memory. All of these lessons and all of these wisdoms, not only for you, but for everyone in this memory is absorbed into your conscious and subconscious minds for your beneficial conscious and beneficial subconscious use. Every detail of this memory in front of you, every aspect, every perception, every understanding, every intent, all of the beneficial absorbed by your perceiving, absorbed by your gesture of this memory. And all of these wisdoms and all of these learning are coming together in your conscious mind and in your subconscious mind for your benefit, for your growth, for your own wisdoms and Understandings.

And as you absorb in any way that you choose to absorb these lessons and wisdoms of benefit, this memory as it is out in front of you, begins to change. As the wisdoms, and the lessons, and the learning's, not only of your own, but of everyone else's and everything else's of this memory is absorbed into your minds. And the memory changes; As all that is left of this memory is of no value, to you, to your conscious, nor to your subconscious mind, still, hanging by the wire, ascended above your timeline, with all of the lessons and learning's and wisdoms removed by your perceptions, removed by your gestures, absorbed into your mind, nothing left of value in this memory, and the wire, or whatever apparatus assisted this memory in ascending to you, continues to cause this memory to ascend, with all of the lessons being gone, all of the wisdoms being gone, that everyone and everything could have, should have, might ought to have learned being taken from this memory, this memory continues to ascend further and further, and further, away from your timeline, going higher and higher as you maintain safely and securely your own position above your past memories, or your own safe bird's eye view of your past memories, and all the things that are left in this memory continuing to ascend further and further over your head, disappearing higher and higher, headed right toward the sun, going further and further away, closer and closer to the sun, until it gets in the sun's gravity where it is pulled into the sun, where it is recycled, where it is joined with the sun's energy, burning itself up in the sun, to continue to add light and warmth for the whole world. You, floating above your timeline with your bird's eye view above your past memories, with all of the wisdoms and learning's from this memory, stored now inside your conscious and subconscious mind, where you can now consciously perceive learning's, consciously judge in wisdom, and all the other wonderful things that conscious can do and subconscious, reinforcing your own conscious choices about your lessons, your wisdoms, your learning's from this memory, and subconscious reinforcing your conscious choice, about other learning's, lessons, wisdoms, from this memory.

Looking down now, on your past timeline, imagine in any way that you choose to imagine or pretend to imagine, that these learning's and wisdoms, these lessons from this past memory, can float right back down to your past timeline, being lessons and learning's, wisdoms, conscious perceptions, understandings and judgments right back down to where this memory ascended from. And watch, or pretend to watch, from your safe place above, as these learning's and wisdoms and lessons all encompassing, of this memory float right back down to this spot on your timeline, among your other past memories, and notice, what happens to your past timeline memories as these learning's take their place once again, in your past memories. Notice your timeline, notice any changes in texture, dimension, lightness or brightness, notice any and all changes as these learning's, wisdoms, lessons and understandings take their place again in your past memories. Notice how these learning's and wisdoms and understanding radiate throughout the rest of your timeline, notice the connectedness of all of your memories. Notice, even, your now, as it is positioned on your timeline in relation to your past, and your future, and notice any changes in your now, with your new learning's, wisdoms, lessons, perceptions and understandings of this memory. And if you have noticed any changes in your timeline, then notice the power that you have as a human being in your mind to change not only your now, but to change your past, to learn, to gain wisdom, not only for yourself and of yourself, but for and of others. Notice the power you have in being human. Now imagine, floating right back above where you are positioned in your present, and from your safe floating position, or from your bird's eye view, looking down to you in your now, noticing you as you are now positioned, with all of the lessons and learning's and wisdoms radiating to your now, radiating even into your tomorrows. Making sure it is you and only you and all of you, imagine floating right back down into you in your present now. And notice how you feel now, notice how you think now, notice sensation, notice awareness's, things that you know that you know, things that you are aware that you are aware of in your present, in your now, and remember your power not only in your now's. Noticing your breath, noticing normal pleasant body sensation, noticing your environment, perceiving with your new lessons and learning's and wisdoms and understandings, open your eyes."

Thank You.

Guided Imagery complete.

CHAPTER 10

OTHER EFFECTS OF ADDICTIONS

We are born without all the programs running in our conscious and subconscious minds. Things like mortal memories aren't in there yet. We are just here as babies and everything we will experience hasn't been experienced yet, so it hasn't been perceived, processed, or stored. Linguistic is a primary process and function, of programing our brain. Just the simple words used around us, within us, by us, simple words and phrases program much of us. The word "yet" presupposes it will happen, "want" indicates a lack of, "of" indicates function, "but" cancels out what was stated prior. Regardless of your conscious thinking of a word, the word does mean what it does mean, in our programming. Things we learn and know can keep coming up for decades after we have learned and know them. Whether we like their coming up or not it's just part of our processes. If we have learned and know them, still they will keep coming up. What we learn and know is part of our programs.

The subconscious just stores and processes the information based on the conscious repeated responses to the information. Whether conscious has access to the information or not is based on conscious responses. I believe we are Eternal Beings. I believe we have and will live forever. I believe we were intelligent beings as spiritual beings prior to receiving our physical bodies. I believe the knowledge of our life before coming to this earth came with us to this earth in each and every one of us. I believe after this life we will continue to live forever. I believe man will be resurrected because of Jesus Christ. I believe when we are resurrected and continue our eternal progression, we will remember this life's experience. It therefore does not make sense to me that each individual as they left heaven to come here had to leave their memories and knowledge of that eternity in heaven.

All dysfunctional behaviors occur when one of the three systems or senses shut down or is in overdrive. Just as with the human body organs when one organ begins to close down, or malfunction, related organs have to pick up the function of the dysfunctional organ.

Negative experiences recorded on Timeline are OK. Though, when the Limbic systems needs information from the Timeline memory, the synaptic nerve endings change to jump across to receptors through the memory storage area, and all negative chemicals are released into the individual's system from that memory. The memory itself is rarely recognized by the individual experiencing the response from this neuron firing in the subconscious.

Negative memories tend to get stuck (stored) together because of the common emotional response, (limbic system, chemicals in common), not because of the common event. For example, emotions of loneliness and hunger are almost the exact identical chemical composition, therefore emotional (response) experience. So an experience of being lonely fires into the limbic system and triggers the same chemical response as being hungry. Therefore, we may eat and feel better from the loneliness. And when we are hungry, we may spend time with a friend and the hunger may go away for a while.

Negative emotional responses are four times more prevalent than positive emotional responses. The dictionary lists approximately 3500 negative emotions and around 2000 positive emotions.

Memories from your pre-birth to now, is your resource file of experiences. If all negatives are in front of self, the negative memory is what will come up first.

Emotions swelling up, one after another is an anxiety attack. Anxiety is a painful or apprehensive uneasiness of mind usually over something impending or anticipated. Anxiety is regarding the future. Your subconscious mind is going back searching for the experience, waiting in the future then searching past finding similar emotions and puts it out in front of you again. Anxiety floats on the TDS Time line.

If you go to find the causes of anxiety it will go away from where you are looking. If you get closer, it will completely leave, causing you to have no conscious idea of any more anxiety. Facing the anxiety will cause it to just disappear.

Fear and apprehension, dread, are also future time-oriented emotions, triggered by negative emotion from the past and projected into the future. Remember, emotions are chemically based and not just memory based or triggered.

Co-dependency is a psychological condition or a relationship where a person is controlled or manipulated by another who is attached with a pathological condition (as an addiction to alcohol or heroin), in short, dependence on the needs of or control by another. Co-dependency is full of guilt. Guilt is full of feeling of blame, culpability, fault, the feeling responsibility for a wrong. Guilt is a past emotion and the past is intended to have action taken regarding it.

Learn and grow from your life's experiences. The Lord gives us nothing we cannot overcome. Every fear, every weakness you perceive you have is a strength inside you waiting to be recognized, trained and perform its function it is here to do.

GUIDED IMAGRY OF THE GIFT

Guided Imagery Dialogue:

"Place yourself in a quiet and comfortable area and position and begin to allow your mind to just wonder. Focusing your conscious thought, simply upon the words, "I wonder," allowing yourself to begin to experience or imagine experiencing "wonder".

Having your eyes closed and focusing upon relaxing your breathing, noticing any sensations as you focus upon, your own thoughts of "wondering".

When you came to this earth you brought a gift for someone in your family. A gift to assist them, to help draw out in them a strength they have within them. A strength they may have forgotten about a strength in something in their life here, may have taken from them through their own life's experiences.

You may have carried this with you for much of your life, wondering what it means, wondering why you have it in you, wondering what you are supposed to do with this.

This is not you, nor Yours, it never was, and it never will be yours. This aspect in you belongs to a family member, maybe a sibling, a parent, your parents or siblings' relationships, perhaps your whole family's relationship with the community or even God.

Someone, in some way within your family, has the strength, the potential, the ability within themselves, something they have never recognized or acknowledged within them.

At times, they may have not understood the aspect of you, this aspect, which is not even you, at all, it's only brought to earth by you to help them recognize their own inner self more.

You may or may not even consciously know yet exact details of this gift you have for them, this aspect of you, which is not you nor is it even yours.

The time is now, the time for you to give this gift to them for them to do as they choose to do with this gift. Time for you to release it, let it go, give it lovingly and caringly to the person or people you brought it here for.

Now, just imagine or pretend to imagine having a container to put this gift in and wrapping this gift, as you choose to wrap it. Imagine or pretend to imagine giving this gift to the person it belongs to.

They may respond in any way you imagine them to respond upon receiving the gift. They may or may not open the gift in front of you, they may or may not even accept the gift from you. You just imagine or pretend to imagine anything as it may happen as you give them the gift.

After giving them the gift, imagine or pretend to imagine saying anything you choose to say to them and remember to thank them for giving you the opportunity to bring them this gift."

Thank you.

Completion of Guided imagery

CHAPTER 11

IDENTITY AND ADDICTIONS

The real "eye" is in the "I" of Identity. What does this little saying truly mean? The "eye" is a light sensitive element of the body which is the image-forming organ of sight. Sight from the eyes is used as the faculty of intellectual or aesthetic perception and appreciation. The word "eye" also indicates something of significance such as the eye of the cut of meat, to be observing and know what is going on, a passage through something. What we actually see is what our own Identity actually is. Not only will you not see in another or your environment anything that isn't already in your own Identity, you will Only Ever See in Others and Your Environments what your own Identity is. This is a closed system.

Identity indicates a sameness of essential or generic character in different instances. Sameness in all that constitutes the objective reality of a thing (As in "Oneness"). So, there is no real objective of a reality for a closed system; the closed systems perception of reality is their own Identity. Identity is the distinguishing character and personality traits of the individual. Identity comes from the relationship established by our psychological Models and Programs of belief about ourselves. We can see nothing beyond our self, the oneness of sameness of Self Identity is the eye, I, is your perceptions. We can only see the sameness of essential or generic character even in completely different instances of a reflection of our character and our own personality. We do not see what we do not identify with. We only see what we identify with. This constitutes the objective reality of all we see. It is all we are. This reality is subjective and is a closed systems reality.

Identity becomes the actual Element of our Being. Identity being the substance creating our reality. An Element is an actual substance which can be put together with other substances and create and compose a variety of things. Therefore, Elements are not complicated because they truly are the simplest principles of and parts of any subject or study. Identity is the primary element, the "eye" of the "needle", (no pun intended), so to speak. The image-forming element organ of all we perceive is our own identity.

You cannot experience something; you don't believe in; you also cannot see something you are not. So, we will only be able to see with our human eye things we already are regarding as our own Identity. This is a closed system.

Identity is the foundation of all we are able to perceive, evaluate, judge and decide about in our conscious mind. A closed systems foundation of their own and others Identity is very consistent and does not change from situation to situation. This foundation might feel and can even appear as a good foundation. Though, you will never learn, change, or grow as a closed system.

All data first goes into the subconscious part of our brain. There, it is processed in a specific pattern in the subconscious. The subconscious is part of an Element or organ of the body, much like other Elements and organs. The way it processes, and Functions does not change from person to person, no more than a heart changes or Functions differently from person to person. All of our systems and organs function as created for human beings and they know their own function, no one had to train them how to work, they already know what to do. Just as our weaknesses become our strengths, it's only a matter of lifting our own self-limiting beliefs (our self-view). Once this occurs, the Element knows it's Function, we just acknowledge it and put it into good use (train it) in our lives.

Our Identity is a Model and Program created through Correspondence between the conscious and subconscious mind.

Once that Identity Model and Program is created, just like all other Models and Programs created throughout our lives. Program's do not go away. There is no way to "change" a subconscious Model or Program and there is no way to make the subconscious Function or Process any differently than the way it is created to Function and Process. You can, however, create New Models and Programs throughout your entire life.

It is stated that Albert Einstein used 10% of his brain. That leaves 90% to still use, to gather data, create and file new Models and Programs. Science has discovered that if the whole central nervous system was taken out of one human being and placed together in a single line of nerves, this line of nerves would go around the earth and out to Jupiter and back several times.

Until our Identity is changed, it's impossible to change what we see, hear, feel, smell, taste, or your intuitions. To perceive, evaluate, judge and decide is all based upon our own Identity with all our own dysfunctional world-views and self-view's limiting beliefs. Yes, the data will go into the subconscious, but it won't be coming up to conscious to be perceived, evaluated judged or decided about. You won't even know it's there until it is a part of the way you view the world and yourself. Until the data does come to conscious for conscious to do its job with the data, there may or may not already be a Model or Program for the subconscious to add the data to. Your conscious processing's is what determines the way the data gets used. The Real "eye" is the "I" of Identity.

The "Identity" of a Closed System becomes the boundaries and limitations that keep the system closed. Oftentimes for the Addict, this becomes lies, stealing, denying, running away and many other hurtful and harmful behaviors, thought patterns and emotional responses.

Again, these are Models and Programs. Can they be changed? No. Though, You can create new Models and Programs and practice using these to make these stronger. Kind of, a natural process in life, though it isn't easy.

Oftentimes, just knowing the Structure, Patterns and Processes of these natural patterns of life may assist us in changing. Scripture indicate that the Lord doesn't give us anything we can't overcome. They speak of giving us weakness so we may know our strengths. These and many scriptures easily explain many natural processes man has discovered about the way the human brain works. The mind's Structure, Patterns and Processes, the different Elements of the human mind and their Functions, the ways they correspond with each other, based upon Physics laws of Similarities and Unity.

God created man in His own image is also stated in the scriptures. The New Testament speaks of many miracles Christ performed during His time on this Earth. In many of these scriptures, Christ tells the people that it is by their Faith that they are healed. When Christ was walking on the water and His apostle wanted to walk with Him. Christ reached out and saved him when he sank into the water and Christ said to him, "Oh ye of little faith."

As a parent or loved one of an addict, what is your Identity of yourself? What is your Identity of your loved one suffering with the addiction? What is the Identity of the addict?

The things your conscious will be allowed to perceive evaluate judge and decide about will all be based upon your "Identity" Models and Programs already created in the subconscious.

Hopeless, helpless is a Closed System and the Identity in a Closed System is the Thoughts, Emotions and Behaviors which keep the system closed.

DISCONTINUOUS DISORDER:

Disorder is a natural part of mortality. Continuous disorder is a repetition of the same behavior over and over again, hoping to have a different response. Disorder is a natural process of life and the Element of Future in the Totality of time is Disorder. If the future was intended for order, there would be no option for Choice nor Change. When disorder becomes a continuous, repeated process of the same disorder over and over again. This is a Closed System.

Discontinuous disorder is an Open System. Disorder is for new experiences and lessons to be learned. Disorder in an open system does not continue, it is overcome, and the open system gains greater knowledge and new identity. Disorder does not just stop coming, this is mortality; to live with disorder, to learn and grow. Disorder itself is an Element of Future time, otherwise the future would be orderly, and we have no future opportunity. Disorder serves a great purpose in our lives for change and for choice. Continuous disorder is in a closed system, while discontinuous disorder is within an open system. The disorder being recognized as it truly is evaluated and judged and decided upon based upon the growth and change of the open system.

Discontinuous Disorder results in constant growth and change. Disorder that comes into a life or a situation and is dealt with by finding a solution to the disorder, this is discontinuous disorder. Overcoming each disorder as it appears and growing and learning with each disorder along life's path. We will not have complete assured order in our lives nor in life's experiences though recognizing, gaining knowledge and new life theories and implementing the theories to express new knowledge is a path we are all capable of walking. Discontinuous Disorder we gain greater knowledge through, overcoming our limiting beliefs of ourselves, gaining wisdoms, strengths, is our purpose of being here.

Permeable boundaries are boundaries of an Open System. The Eye of the open system can see all the data and feedback in its entire environment. Open systems can see the unforeseeable, unforeseen and the un-foretold. An open system Identity "eye", perception becomes beyond all expectation of possibilities and observes beyond limited boundaries. Unpredictable "Eye" Identity, with the boundaries of their perception reflecting; the unpredictable, unforeseeable, unforeseen and unforetold feedback from their environment.

Identity of an Open System is unpredictable it varies and changes with all it sees. Open Systems are very rare human beings. Being open to any and all feedback and data from their environment serves to bring them great knowledge and wisdom. Open Systems discern many things about their self and others they observe the unobservable, they recognize the unrecognizable in others and in the world around them. Open Systems have access to their own knowing which may at times surprise even them how easily it just comes to their conscious mind. Each experience an Open System has is a learning experience and having discovered the more it learns the more there is to learn. An Open System has a multitude of options of dealing with life's problems and often have themselves already prepared for them even before they came. Disorder in the life of an Open System is discontinuous because personal wisdom and knowledge just grows automatically.

Again, being an open system surrounded by closed systems takes wisdom, choice and time; open system is an on-going process which is a natural part of being an open system. Open systems think, feel and do differently with each life experience, they communicate, overcome and grow regardless "of" the challenge placed upon them.

Just practice observing; hearing and seeing what is going on in your environment not evaluating or judging it yet. Just observe your environment. This can be difficult with so many closed systems around you judging for you, evaluating for you. Let them judge, evaluate, and even decide. However, not for you.

FIRST ELEMENT OF BEING AN OPEN SYSTEM:

ADMIT FEEDBACK THROUGH SYSTEM BOUNDARIES INTERCHANGABLEY.

An Open System Admits Feedback from its environment into its system and transmits Feedback from its system back into the environment freely. Open Systems have a unified field of consciousness for all the feedback in its field. This unified field is Holographic and identifiable by the illustration below. Admit just means to PERMIT, to allow scope for, to allow entry into. Feedback is Admitted and given back into the environment through the systems boundaries around the system. So Feedback from the environment is acknowledged, recognized, admitted into and out of the systems boundaries.

Holographical, as it pertains to the Holographic Human Transformation Theory is only referring to the sense of sound and sight through the systems boundaries. All there are to Admit into the systems boundaries is what is heard and seen in the systems environment. What is heard and what is seen is the category for what is referred to as Feedback from and back into the systems environment. This Admit process is only a Mental process, an awareness of what is heard and seen in the environment. Simply acknowledging, recognizing and allowing it into the system itself. It's really just this simple. The difficult aspect is in controlling our own conscious nature and NOT jumping into evaluating, judging and deciding about what the system hears and sees. The boundaries are permeable. Evaluating, judging and deciding is not up to the system boundaries. Awareness is the specific function of system boundaries. It is one thing to know the truth of what is going on in your environment and an Open System does recognize and know their environment. Boundaries of the system are not about what the system will and will not tolerate, boundaries of an Open System is about what the system sees and hears from its environment. Perceiving, being able to see and hear the reality of our environments helps us to see and hear the unforeseen, the unforetold. Once this Element of an Open System is attained or accomplished, the other 2 Elements of the Open System then do their Function and Process. Without the 1st Element being implemented there is no reality, no "Eye" in Identity for the system to function properly. This is the same Function and process of the boundaries of the Open System after the system has completed its internal system process and is ready to Express its "Eye" Identity back into its environment through the same system boundaries. It Expresses its Feedback in ways that the environment can see and hear for itself the Expression from the Open System to its input.

So the boundaries of an Open System just Admits the Feedback correspondingly between the system and its environment.

SECOND ELEMENT OF BEING AN OPEN SYSTEM:

ACCEPT THE FEEDBACK FROM THE ENVIORNMENT.

Accept the Data, dialogue the Data. Experience the Dialogue of the Data. Create New Theories of the new Data, Dialogue and Experiences. The Function and process of Accept is simply taking the sounds and sights from the environment and either writing or mentally putting the Data together in a written dialogue format. As simple as this example: I heard a dog bark and a male voice yell for the dog to stop barking. At the same time, I saw a blue truck and heard it honk its horn. I saw the man who yelled at the dog run toward the barking dog, and the truck veered to miss hitting the dog, and the truck hit the fire hydrant.

Using all of the Data from the environment and writing or putting it together into an information and informative format. This process is of Evaluating the Data from the environment for the purpose of discovering theories for the system to consider implementing. Judging and Deciding is Not a part of the Theory process of this Element of Accept the Data in an Open System. The dialogue is created without prejudice or opinion, just as facts of what is and was heard and seen. This dialogue is looked at objectively and new theories considered to implement in response to the dialogue. The Feedback from the systems environment is intended for the growth of the system, especially when the Feedback is repetitive in the environment. The Open system responds to the feedback only after the open system has formatted the feedback into information for the system, come up with new theories of ways for the system to deal with the feedback and then implements the new theories.

The Theory process is just the facts and circumstances of what is seen and heard used in a phrase. This is an abstract thought that has yet to be proven. Such as in the barking dog example; the theory might be that people do not enjoy hitting dogs.

THIRD ELEMENT OF AN OPEN SYSTEM:

EXPRESS.

This process is physical and future processes, shown through our behaviors, our character, and our strategies. This is the implementation of the information we have gathered and gaining knowledge through implementing the new theories from the information. This is experience and sharing as well as living our lives by these experiences. Returning our learning's and understanding back to the environment while remaining open to further information, new theories and processes to implement these. This being a third element consists of the ending of the cycle of the three elements of an open system and a new beginning of a continuation of being an open system.

Each time through gaining more knowledge to implement and express back into the environment while receiving new information and new theories to implement by way of expressing through behaviors, beliefs, processes, strategies and function. This is where conscious judges and decides and starts the perceiving function again.

ELEMENTS OF MEMORY:

* Real Memory: Used to create our Identity and our Personality.

* Vicarious Memory: Used to create our Emotional Response and our Communication Processes.

* Genetic Memory: Used to create our Core Beliefs of self, functions, and strategies.

The Conscious

A Whole Bit of information consists of:

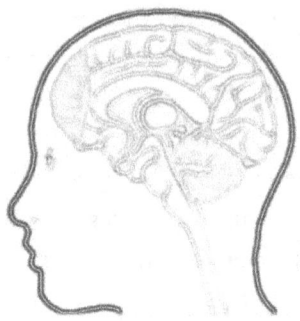

Content : raw data

Context : information that gives data meaning

Intent : a direction of action.

Three different decisions are available from each whole bit
1. Take Action
2. Let Someone Else Take Action
3. Do Nothing

The Subconscious

Filters information for conscious use:

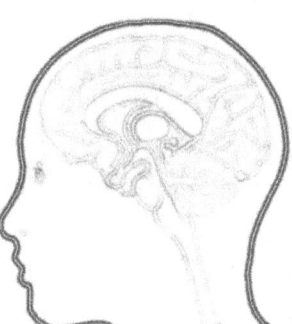

The subconscious filters sensory information in a pattern called a meta program.

Meta programs filter by deleting, distorting or generalizing information by sense. The info then may come up to conscious awareness.

Meta programs themselves may function beyond conscious awareness, however.

Repeat the assignments in this book, practice implementing your increased knowledge.

Read and re-read the new information in this book so you may also understand and express it in your life's experience.

Learning more of this information and Holographic Human Transformation Theory may offer you, assistance in overcoming your mortal programs. Which in turn, may help you be more open to the Gospel teachings and principles and become the "you", you are able to be.

Glossary:

Accepted -merely means that the acknowledgment of it is dialogued internally within an Open System itself (you) and New Theories of what it might mean and what might be the best approach to dealing with it followed with discussion of this with the Closed System

Addicted - means to devote or surrender oneself, to something habitually or obsessively, to be addicted means to commit by a solemn act, often times by compelling motives and attachment to an objective. A habit is the prevailing disposition or character of a person's thoughts, feelings and behaviors. Our thoughts, feelings and behaviors are committed by solemn act and compelling motives and attachment to the object we are addicted to. Nothing else really matters. Not others, not the self, addiction is like cancer and like cancer can kill the addict.

Addiction – Addiction is a compulsive need for and use of a behavior or habit-forming substance characterized by tolerance and by well-defined physiological symptoms upon withdrawal.

Addiction on a mental level - Addictions on a Mental level may appear as innocent seeming thought patterns, perceptions with strong opinions. These thought patterns can become very harmful, even destructive to oneself and others.

Addictions on an Emotional level - are habitual emotional responses which can also harm the self and others.

Addictions on a Physical level - are the most obvious and judged by others. Addiction on this level can be illegal and even cause death.

Addictive System- Systems that are closed to natural forms of feedback become Addictive systems

Admitted - merely means here the acknowledgment, perception, actually seeing and hearing what the addict says, how the addict feels and what the addict does.

Anomalies - Anomalies is information that runs counter to the commons (beliefs, norms), There anomalies are actually built into the system from the start. Anomalies deviate from the rules and guidelines turning counter to the whole purpose. Anomalies are inconsistent with or deviating from what is usual, normal, or expected. An anomaly is "uncertain of nature or classification" and is deviating from the norm.

Closed System - An addictive system. It becomes nothing more than the very boundaries and limitations to keep the system closed. The actual identity of the person just seems to vanish and all that appears to be left of them are the foundation of the addiction. Our whole identity seems to become the thoughts feelings and behaviors that help tolerate the addiction.

Codependency - is a psychological condition or a relationship where a person is controlled or manipulated by another who is attached with a pathological condition (as an addiction to alcohol or heroin), in short dependence on the needs of or control by another. Codependency is full of guilt. Guilt is full of feeling of blame, culpability, fault, the feeling responsibility for a wrong

Educate - To draw out.

Elements - Separate entities with their own identity and function that work with other elements through correspondence working interdependently and interrelated to make a whole.

Entropy - is considered a measure of the unavailable energy in a Closed System that is also usually considered to be the measure of the systems disorder. The function of the entropy is to the ultimate state of inert uniformity, a lacking of the power to move. A deficient in active properties due to the lacking of usual or anticipated actions, simple put the entropy (*unavailable energy) is unskilled. The entropy released its available energy in an effort to avoid change due to being unskilled to change itself.

Expressed - is merely the consistent, repeated doing of the "what might be the best" approach to dealing with what was acknowledged and perceived

"I am" statements - are Identity Level statements.

Meta Programs - Major Meta Programs: Memory, Time, Identity, Communication, Wisdom, Family, just to list a few.

Open System – Open systems are systems that take in feedback, data, and information from its environment and surroundings and processes these.

Permeable -Penetrable.

Quantum's -Mind, emotions (spirit) body have two quantum leaps each.

1. Right
2. God
3. Life
4. Wrong
5. Self
6. Death.

Refusal - The turning down of a proposal. Rejection disapproval, refusing to accept internal promptings, let alone outside feedback. The act of refusing rejecting, disapproving and just giving up. The opposite of Refuse is Acceptance.

Repression - Countermeasure, against, revolt. Clamp down, suppression, pacification. The action or processes of repressing and the state of being repressed. A mental process by which distressing thoughts memories or impulses that may give rise to anxiety are excluded from consciousness and left to operate in the subconscious. Put down or prevent natural development.

Stability - becomes dysfunctional because a Closed System can only duplicate itself, therefore Closed Systems become generational.

TDS - Trans Derivational Search - A multi-directional search for information throughout all the body systems.

Tolerance - What happens with an addiction regarding tolerance is it takes more and more of the behaviors and or substances because of "tolerance", to get the same response to ease the compelling motives regarding the objective of the addiction. The objective of the addiction isn't the substance, is it the responsive feeling of escape from the self. The self never goes away in this life or in the life to come and the addiction isn't the answer to the hatred and humiliation of self.

Totality- Is a whole system. When all systems are open and corresponding together, we have the Whole system's identity.

Unbridgeability - Unbridgeability is about choices, choice is a quantum leap syndrome. Be willing to let go to be one with self and God and move to goals, nurture self when others are not willing to choose to go with you, they choose to stay.

Quantum's:

1) Right and Wrong - Mind
2) God and Self - Emotions or Spirit
3) Life and Death - Body

Each level: (Mind, Emotions or Spirit and Body have 2 quantum leaps each).

About the Author

Janey Marvin researched the second law of thermal dynamics applying the laws and principles of the closed system for more than a decade. She applied the physics laws and principles to her know of human behaviors and patterns. This research work began for in in the early 1990's, having been introduced by Paradigm theory by Thomas Kuhn. The Open and Closed System book has been implemented into the educational and experiential program for substance abuse and mental health treatment since the company she and a business partner incorporated in 1993. With much success with the clients changing their lives, many clients creating new pathways for their families and overcoming their addiction, this theory matches very well with problems faces as human beings. Janey has a special way of taking words, experiences, observations, as literal and breaks them down from there. Janey has had many challenges in her life, recently, a difficult one being the disappearance of her oldest son, Joshua Simiskey. Through this and other difficulties, Janey has grown and overcome and continued to be able to help herself and help others by knowing this information, taking it literally and implementing it;s application into her thoughts, feelings and life experiences.

www.ingramcontent.com/pod-product-compliance
Lightning Source LLC
LaVergne TN
LVHW011712060526
838200LV00051B/2871